SKILLS & VALUES:
THE FIRST AMENDMENT

SKILLS & VALUES:
THE FIRST AMENDMENT

Second Edition

Charles W. "Rocky" Rhodes
Professor of Law
South Texas College of Law

Paul E. McGreal
Dean and Professor of Law
University of Dayton School of Law

 LexisNexis

ISBN: 978-0-7698-6376-4
eBook ISBN: 978-0-3271-8527-7

Library of Congress Cataloging-in-Publication Data

Rhodes, Charles W.
    Skills & values: The First Amendment / Charles W. "Rocky" Rhodes, professor of law, South Texas College of Law,
    Paul E. McGreal, dean and professor of law, University of Dayton School of Law. -- Second edition.
        pages cm.
    Includes index.
    ISBN 978-0-7698-6376-4
    1. United States. Constitution 1st Amendment--Problems, exercises, etc. 2. Freedom of speech--United States--Problems,
    exercises, etc. 3. Freedom of the press--United States--Problems, exercises, etc. 4. Freedom of religion--United States--
    Problems, exercises, etc. I. McGreal, Paul E. II. Bergin, Kathleen A. Skills & values. First Amendment. III. Title. IV.
    Title: First Amendment. V. Title: Skills and values.
        KF4770.B39 2013
        342.7308'52--dc23
    2013023702

NOTE TO USERS
To ensure that you are using the latest materials available in this area, please be sure to periodically check the LexisNexis Law School web site for downloadable updates and supplements at www.lexisnexis.com/lawschool.

Editorial Offices
121 Chanlon Rd., New Providence, NJ 07974 (908) 464-6800
201 Mission St., San Francisco, CA 94105-1831 (415) 908-3200
www.lexisnexis.com

MATTHEW◆BENDER

PREFACE

This book allows you to experience the connection between theory, doctrine, and practice in First Amendment law. The exercises provide an opportunity for studying First Amendment concepts from the perspective of a practicing attorney who must not only know the law, but also employ lawyering skills and values — such as legal strategy, factual development, advocacy, counseling, drafting, problem solving, and ethical principles — in zealously representing a client.

Each chapter addresses a specific topic covered in most First Amendment law school courses. The chapters begin with an introduction that helps bridge the gap between the actual practice of law and the doctrine and theory you studied in class. You will then have an opportunity to engage in active, "hands on" learning by working through a stand-alone exercise that simulates a real-life legal dilemma. The exercises are as authentic as possible, incorporating materials such as legal pleadings, motions, correspondence, judicial opinions, statutes, discovery materials, and deposition excerpts. Each exercise explains your role, lists the tasks you are required to perform, details the practice skills needed, provides an estimated completion time, has a level of difficulty based on a scale of 1 to 5, and contains pertinent statutes or regulations. Some exercises also include practice tips that highlight important issues or litigation strategies a competent First Amendment lawyer would want to consider.

The book can be used in a number of different ways. Your professor might ask you to complete the tasks in each exercise and produce the assigned written documents for a grade or constructive feedback. Depending on the size and structure of the class, the book might alternatively be used for in-class exercises that you are instructed to complete individually or as part of a group. You can also use the book on your own to reinforce substantive lessons from class and hone important practice skills.

You may also want to use the LexisNexis Web Course that was created for this book, which contains forms to assist you in completing some of the exercises, audio and video files, links to some of the key cases, and other supplemental materials designed to increase your understanding of both doctrine and practice. We hope that you find both the book and the platform enjoyable and useful to your development of lawyering skills and values.

Charles W. "Rocky" Rhodes
Houston, Texas

Paul E. McGreal
Dayton, Ohio

TABLE OF CONTENTS

Chapter 1	INCITEMENT OF ILLEGAL ACTIVITY	**1**
Exercise 1		3
Chapter 2	OBSCENITY AND SEXUALLY EXPLICIT MATERIAL	**9**
Exercise 2		12
Chapter 3	THE FIGHTING WORDS DOCTRINE	**19**
Exercise 3		22
Chapter 4	COMMERCIAL SPEECH	**23**
Exercise 4		27
Chapter 5	LIBEL, DEFAMATION, AND OTHER TORTS	**31**
Exercise 5		34
Chapter 6	TIME, PLACE, AND MANNER RESTRICTIONS	**37**
Exercise 6		40
Chapter 7	VAGUENESS AND OVERBREADTH	**45**
Exercise 7		48
Chapter 8	PUBLIC EMPLOYEE SPEECH RIGHTS	**51**
Exercise 8		55
Chapter 9	PUBLIC SCHOOL STUDENTS' SPEECH RIGHTS	**57**
Exercise 9		59
Chapter 10	GOVERNMENT SPEECH	**63**
Exercise 10		66
Chapter 11	FREEDOM OF EXPRESSIVE ASSOCIATION	**69**
Exercise 11		71
Chapter 12	THE POLITICAL PROCESS AND THE FIRST AMENDMENT	**75**
Exercise 12		77
Chapter 13	THE NEWSGATHERING FUNCTION AND FREEDOM OF THE PRESS	**79**
Exercise 13		82

TABLE OF CONTENTS

Chapter 14   **THE ESTABLISHMENT CLAUSE** **87**

   Exercise 14 90

Chapter 15   **THE FREE EXERCISE CLAUSE** **93**

   Exercise 15 96

Chapter 1

INCITEMENT OF ILLEGAL ACTIVITY

INTRODUCTION

The cases addressing incitement of illegal activity usually arise in one of three situations. First, sometimes a prosecution is based on speech or symbolic expression made by a "rabble rouser" in public who is trying to whip a crowd into a frenzy to engage in some illegal activity. This has occasionally arisen in the context of a group embracing racial superiority principles, such as the Aryan Nations or the Ku Klux Klan. It has also occurred in protests that started peaceably, but then a protestor or group of protestors encouraged others to engage in illegal activities, including assaults, trespass, or property destruction. These cases typically reach an attorney after an arrest of the rabble rouser who then must be prosecuted or defended.

The second situation involves more surreptitious activities, in which an organization attempts to develop subversive plans in secret. This may occur with an anarchist or terrorist group that has designs to overthrow the government of the United States. For instance, after the 9/11 attacks, the government claims groups of radical jihadists met secretly in the United States to recruit members and raise funds to join with foreign terrorist organizations in launching attacks against the United States. During the Cold War, there were similar contentions that groups of Communists were secretly spreading Marxist dogma that would then be used at the appropriate time to overthrow the government of the United States. Due to the secrecy of these organizations and their violent objectives, the government sometimes is faced with a dilemma — either move in quickly and face the risk that only abstract teaching protected by the First Amendment rather than unprotected preparation for violent action has occurred, or wait and face the risk that the organization may accomplish its objectives.

The final scenario involves the publication or dissemination of materials that either contain or depict romanticism of violence or instructions for committing unlawful acts. A key question in these cases is the speaker's intent. A song, for example, may praise the virtues of suicide, or the thrill of killing a police officer, but if the performer did not intend that the viewers or listeners commit an act of violence, it is protected under the First Amendment. This protection is lost only in those rare situations in which the performer or publisher has the intent either to incite the audience into likely, imminent unlawful acts or to aid and abet the commission of a criminal offense. *Cf. Rice v. Paladin Enterprises, Inc.*, 128 F.3d 233, 242–50 (4th Cir. 1997).

After decades of struggling with the appropriate legal approach to employ in these and similar situations, the Supreme Court pronounced the governing standard for incitement of illegal activity in *Brandenburg v. Ohio*, 395 U.S. 444 (1969).

1

Brandenburg addressed the constitutionality of a Ku Klux Klan leader's conviction under Ohio's criminal syndicalism statute for advocating unlawful acts of violence as a means to accomplish political reform. While recognizing that it had upheld the constitutionality of a similar syndicalism statute in *Whitney v. California*, 274 U.S. 357 (1927), the *Brandenburg* Court viewed *Whitney* as having been "thoroughly discredited by [its] later decisions." The Court reasoned that its more recent decisions required a distinction between "the mere abstract teaching" of the need for lawlessness or violence and the actual preparation of a group for violent or unlawful action. 395 U.S. at 447-48. As a result, the Court declared that the government may not "forbid or proscribe advocacy of the use of force or of law violation except where such advocacy is directed to inciting or producing imminent lawless action and is likely to produce such action." *Id.* at 447.

Brandenburg's incitement test contains three basic elements: (1) the speaker must intend to incite or produce unlawful action, (2) the unlawful action must be imminent, and (3) the unlawful action must be likely to occur. Subsequent decisions confirm that an intent for, and an immediacy and probability of, lawless action are all necessary before an expressive exhortation can be subject to criminal sanction. In *Hess v. Indiana*, 414 U.S. 105 (1973), for instance, the Supreme Court overturned a protestor's conviction for stating, as the police were clearing an anti-war demonstration from a public street, that "We'll take the fucking street later." The Court reasoned that, since his statement was not directed at any particular person or group, the requisite intent to advocate action was missing. Moreover, his words were neither directed to produce, nor likely to produce, imminent disorder. Similarly, in *NAACP v. Claiborne Hardware Co.*, 458 U.S. 886, 927-29 (1982), the Court determined that a civil rights leader's incendiary rhetoric urging a boycott of white merchants, including the possibility of breaking the necks of those refusing to participate and the impossibility of round-the-clock police protection for boycott violators, was protected under the First Amendment when no violence occurred until weeks later.

But the Supreme Court has only rarely addressed incitement of illegal activity since *Brandenburg*. The following exercise provides an opportunity for you to apply its test.

EXERCISE 1

You are a United States Attorney working with the Federal Bureau of Investigation regarding an ongoing investigation of Ali Hussein Laden, a United States citizen living in Alexandria, Virginia who is under surveillance due to his suspected links to the terrorist organization al Qaeda. The FBI wants you to prosecute Laden for treason if doing so would not violate the First Amendment.

The FBI periodically brings you the information it has obtained through public records and through an informant regarding Laden's activities in the days following September 11, 2001. The FBI then wants you to prepare an indictment (which is similar to a complaint in a civil case) against Laden for treason, if there is sufficient information to establish probable cause. The Bureau also wants your written opinion regarding whether Laden's activities are protected by the First Amendment and whether the arrest should be delayed to obtain additional evidence that will be necessary to ensure a conviction.

REQUIRED TASKS FOR EACH BLOG ENTRY OR REPORT:

Task 1: Prepare an indictment for treason if sufficient information exists to do so in compliance with a prosecutor's ethical obligations under Rule 3.8 of the Model Rules of Professional Conduct (the LexisNexis Web Course contains a form for the indictment that has been started for you, and there is a completed indictment that you may review in Exercise 11).

Task 2: Prepare a memo on whether Laden's activities are protected by the First Amendment.

Task 3: Advise in your memo whether the arrest should be delayed to obtain additional evidence that will be necessary to ensure a conviction.

PRACTICE SKILLS UTILIZED:

Skill 1: Constitutional and statutory analysis
Skill 2: Critical reasoning from cases
Skill 3: Criminal pleading
Skill 4: Strategic thinking

ESTIMATED TIME FOR COMPLETION: Approximately 1 hour per entry

LEVEL OF DIFFICULTY (1 TO 5):

PERTINENT CONSTITUTIONAL, STATUTORY, AND ETHICAL PROVISIONS:

United States Constitution Article III, § 3:

> Treason against the United States, shall consist only in levying War against them, or in adhering to their Enemies, giving them Aid and Comfort. No Person shall be convicted of Treason unless on the Testimony of two Witnesses to the same overt Act, or on Confession in open Court.

18 U.S.C. § 2381: Treason

> Whoever, owing allegiance to the United States, levies war against them or adheres to their enemies, giving them aid and comfort within the United States or elsewhere, is guilty of treason and shall suffer death, or shall be imprisoned not less than five years and fined under this title but not less than $10,000, and shall be incapable of holding any office under the United States.

Model Rule of Professional Conduct 3.8: Special Responsibilities of a Prosecutor

> The prosecutor in a criminal case shall (a) refrain from prosecuting a charge that the prosecutor knows is not supported by probable cause; . . .

Practice Tip: After carefully analyzing the constitutional and statutory elements of treason, you may want to supplement your understanding with case law research. You also will need to pay careful attention to how to prove all these elements, especially considering the need for testimony from two witnesses to the same overt act. The ethical rules require that you cannot proceed if you know that the charge is not supported by probable cause, which is essentially a reasonable ground for belief that the charge is warranted under the law and the presented facts.

9/12/01

ALI HUSSEIN LADEN
FOUNDER
THE CENTER FOR ISLAM

Praise to Allah!

Yesterday, the World witnessed the deserved retribution against America for its crimes against our way of life!

Upon hearing the news of the destruction of the two towers of the World Trade Center yesterday, my heart felt good omens that I had to spread to my brothers. This is a strong signal that Western supremacy (especially that of America) is coming to a quick end, God Willing, as occurred to these buildings.

The attacks yesterday were justified under our fatwas. Their success indicates that the End of Time battle has begun. Be prepared in spirit for this new struggle!

Join me tonight at the Center as I discuss these events and how the End of Time battle has been foretold!

THE EXERCISE:

The FBI Informant reveals that Laden was joined by three dozen followers that night at the Center. During the meeting, he described the sacred religious rulings, or fatwas, that he believed justified the 9/11 attacks, and then he ended with the following prayer:

> Oh, Allah, destroy America. Slay the unbelievers wherever you find them. Let death come to them by the hands of the holy fighters. And help more to answer the call to this fight.

Complete the assigned tasks based on Laden's 9/12/01 conduct.

<u>www.laden.com.blogspot</u>   9/13/01

ALI HUSSEIN LADEN
FOUNDER
THE CENTER FOR ISLAM

The first stages of jihad are upon us. The Western world, including America, should be stabbed until it bleeds to death.

The Taliban in Afghanistan is preparing for an assault by the infidels. They need our support and our prayers. They need holy fighters to prevail in this jihad.

Join me tonight at the Center to pray for victory in this struggle!

THE EXERCISE:

At the Center that night, the FBI informant explains that Laden was joined by approximately a dozen of his followers. Most of the meeting consisted of prayers and the recitation of verses and religious rulings that Laden believed justified jihad.

After the meeting concluded, Laden approached six of his followers individually. He asked them to join with him the next night at his home for further study of the justness of the cause. The informant was one of the six who was invited to Laden's home.

Complete the assigned tasks based on Laden's 9/13/01 conduct.

Transcript of Informant's 9/14/01 Report on Ali Hussein Laden

I went to Laden's house about 7 p.m. As I approached, I noticed that the house was entirely dark, with all the shades pulled down. I knocked on the door, and then it was opened. Four people were inside, including Laden. The room was illuminated only by a few candles. Laden then approached me and asked for my cell phone, which I handed to him.

Another two people came to the door shortly thereafter. Laden asked for their cell phones as well, which they handed over. He then placed all the cell phones in a small lock box in the entry way, and had us walk with him into the living area of his home.

He began by stating that we were all alone, cut off from the outside world. No cell phones, no electricity — he had even cut the phone lines to his house. He needed our meeting to be as secretive as possible due to its great urgency.

He said he wanted us to travel abroad and join the Taliban in fighting against the American troops. Of all of his followers, he believed we were the most worthy, and we would obtain salvation by fighting in the jihad. He asked each of us if we would agree to do so. All six of us agreed. He told us to return tomorrow evening and he would provide us with instructions on how to travel to Pakistan and join al Qaeda without being detected by the authorities.

THE EXERCISE:

After showing you this transcript, the FBI wants you to complete the assigned tasks for 9/14/01.

Transcript of Informant's 9/15 Report on Ali Hussein Laden

I returned to Laden's house this evening at 7 p.m. Everything was the same as the night before — the house was dark, Laden collected all the cell phones, and we joined in his living room.

But on this occasion it was all business. Laden had prepared detailed instructions regarding how we each should proceed to join the Taliban. The instructions explained step-by-step how to obtain the travel visas that we would need to get to Pakistan and what to say when we were asked the purpose of our travel.

Laden said that, after we obtained the travel visas, we should travel by train to New York City. From there we should fly to Pakistan. Once we got to Pakistan, an al Qaeda operative would meet us and then escort us to Afghanistan to assist the Taliban cause against the United States.

THE EXERCISE:

Complete the assigned tasks for 9/15/01.

Chapter 2

OBSCENITY AND SEXUALLY EXPLICIT MATERIAL

INTRODUCTION

Restrictions on sexually explicit material typically take one of two forms: (1) a flat prohibition on the production, sale, or distribution of obscenity; or (2) the regulation of adult businesses that are sexually explicit though not obscene. Lawmakers are free to restrict or even ban obscenity because it is not protected speech under the First Amendment. Measures that burden the operation of adult businesses, however, will be subject to intermediate scrutiny under the "secondary effects" doctrine.

Miller v. California, 413 U.S. 15 (1973), defined obscenity as material that depicts or describes "patently offensive" sexual conduct that is specifically set forth by applicable law. The material must both appeal to the "prurient interest" when viewed as a whole by the average person, and lack serious literary, artistic, political, or scientific value. Whether the material is patently offensive and appeals to the prurient interest is judged by a "contemporary community standard." Whether it lacks serious value is judged by a nation-wide reasonable person standard.

In practice, it is sometimes difficult to identify the relevant "community" whose values determine whether the material is exceedingly prurient or offensive. In *Miller*, the Court rejected a claim of constitutional error based on the prosecution's failure to offer evidence of a national standard, and affirmed the trial court's instructions that the jury consider state-wide attitudes. According to Chief Justice Burger, differences in people's taste and temperament make it impossible to ascertain a uniform national standard of obscenity. Though the First Amendment protects some explicit material, he explained, it does not require "that the people of Maine or Mississippi accept public depictions of conduct found tolerable in Las Vegas, or New York City." *Id.* at 32. This means that what is obscene in one jurisdiction might not be obscene in another.

Application of a state-wide standard is not *required*, however, and later cases made clear that the fact-finder is permitted to "draw on knowledge of the community or vicinage from which [it] comes." *Hamling v. United States*, 418 U.S. 87, 104 (1974). In some cases, a state statute might require that the jury consider the community values of the county or judicial district where the offense is committed. Other statutes might reference a generic "community standard," in which case you may have an opportunity to request jury instructions that clarify the scope of inquiry. In any obscenity case, therefore, a prosecutor can increase the likelihood of conviction by determining which venues are proper, and filing charges in the most conservative one.

Today, of course, most obscene material is distributed over the Internet, and courts have split on the issue of whether a national community standard should apply in online obscenity cases. *Compare U.S. v. Little*, 2010 U.S. App. LEXIS 2320 (11th Cir. Feb. 2, 2010), *with U.S. v. Kilbride*, 584 F.3d 1240 (2009). The Supreme Court has recognized the right of adults to access online content that might be inappropriate for minors, but has not squarely addressed the community standards issue as it relates to the Internet. *See ACLU v. Ashcroft*, 535 U.S. 564 (2002); *Reno v. ACLU*, 521 U.S. 844 (1997). Given the world-wide access to the Internet, and the inability to geographically restrict availability of potentially obscene material, the fear is that applying a local community standard would force content-providers to abide by the preferences of the least tolerant community. To paraphrase *Miller*, people accessing the Internet in New York City and Las Vegas will only find material acceptable to the people of Maine and Mississippi.

Regardless of how one defines the relevant community, the Court has explained that certain depictions will *not* be obscene. In *Jenkins v. Georgia*, 418 U.S. 153 (1974), the Court held as a matter of law that the film *Carnal Knowledge* did not meet the *Miller* obscenity test. The Supreme Court explained its conclusion as follows:

> While the subject matter of the picture is, in a broader sense, sex, and there are scenes in which sexual conduct including "ultimate sexual acts" is to be understood to be taking place, the camera does not focus on the bodies of the actors at such times. There is no exhibition whatever of the actors' genitals, lewd or otherwise, during these scenes. There are occasional scenes of nudity, but nudity alone is not enough to make material legally obscene under the *Miller* standards.

Id. at 161. This passage provides two reference points in further defining obscenity. First, a depiction of nudity, standing alone, does not make a work obscene. Second, a depiction that implies sexual conduct, even "ultimate sexual acts," also does not itself make a work obscene. These two conclusions provide concrete examples that advocates can use to analogize or distinguish future cases.

Unlike the first two *Miller* prongs, the third prong relies on a national reasonable person standard to determine whether the material as a whole lacks "serious literary, artistic, political or scientific value." *Pope v. Illinois*, 481 U.S. 497 (1987). On the one hand, this prong expands the scope of the First Amendment by protecting speech that is otherwise prurient or patently offensive under the relevant community standard. On the other hand, only material with *serious* value is protected; prurient and patently offensive material that has *some* social value is still obscene.

The government not only has the power to ban obscenity under *Miller*, it can also restrict the operation of sexually explicit adult businesses under the "secondary effects" doctrine. Measures designed to stabilize property values and reduce the risk of crime and sexually transmitted disease are deemed to be "content neutral" even when they apply to adult businesses exclusively. Under the applicable intermediate scrutiny standard, a city might concentrate adult theaters within a particular geographic location or limit the proximity of one theater to another without violating the First Amendment. *See Renton v. Playtime Theatres*, 475 U.S. 41 (1986). It might even ban one particular form of adult expression, nude dancing for instance, so long as alternative means of communicating the underlying erotic message are available. *See Erie v. Pap's A.M.*, 529 U.S. 277 (2000).

The Supreme Court has also held that the government need not produce its own evidence of secondary effects. For example, in *Renton*, a city set a buffer zone between adult businesses and residential neighborhoods, schools, parks, and churches. The city asserted that the ordinance targeted the secondary effects of adult businesses on surrounding areas, and thus was not aimed at suppressing speech. The city, however, relied on evidence of secondary effects from other cities rather than conducting its own research into whether such effects existed within its borders. The Supreme Court explained that a city may rely on such evidence in support of secondary effects:

> We hold that Renton was entitled to rely on the experiences of Seattle and other cities, and in particular on the "detailed findings" summarized in the Washington Supreme Court's *Northend Cinema* opinion, in enacting its adult theater zoning ordinance. The First Amendment does not require a city, before enacting such an ordinance, to conduct new studies or produce evidence independent of that already generated by other cities, so long as whatever evidence the city relies upon is reasonably believed to be relevant to the problem that the city addresses. That was the case here. Nor is our holding affected by the fact that Seattle ultimately chose a different method of adult theater zoning than that chosen by Renton, since Seattle's choice of a different remedy to combat the secondary effects of adult theaters does not call into question either Seattle's identification of those secondary effects or the relevance of Seattle's experience to Renton.

Renton, 475 U.S. at 52.

Practice Tip: The Supreme Court has declined to formally expand the "secondary effects" doctrine beyond cases that involve adult entertainment. *See, e.g., Boos v. Barry*, 485 U.S. 312, 320–21 (1988) (declining to extend secondary effects doctrine to ban on picket signs within 500 feet of a foreign embassy). The doctrine has been applied by lower federal courts in other circumstances, however. *See, e.g., Long v. Board of Education of Jefferson County*, 121 F. Supp. 2d 621, 624–25 (W.D. Ky. 2000) (identifying "gang activity" as dangerous secondary effect that justified student dress code).

EXERCISE 2

Your client, Devon Herschild, is the owner of Rest Easy Hotels. She is served with a summons and criminal complaint that charges her with violating certain provisions of the state code. She wants to know whether the charges are legitimate, and whether she can proceed with plans to open a new hotel in a busy downtown area without violating the law.

Herschild brings you a copy of the charging document, along with a letter she received from Citizens for Community Values. How do you advise her?

REQUIRED TASKS:

Task 1:   Draft a Motion to Dismiss asserting all appropriate grounds for relief (the LexisNexis Web Course contains a form for the motion that has been started for you).

Task 2:   Identify facts that may help or harm your client in a future obscenity prosecution.

Task 3:   Provide client advice to mitigate the risk of future litigation.

PRACTICE SKILLS UTILIZED:

Skill 1:   Statutory analysis and case law research
Skill 2:   Motion drafting
Skill 3:   Factual development
Skill 4:   Creative problem solving

ESTIMATED TIME FOR COMPLETION: Approximately 1 hour

LEVEL OF DIFFICULTY (1 TO 5):

State of Astoria	District Court
County of New Yonkers	Fifth Judicial District
	Court File No. 742

State of Astoria,
              Plaintiff,

[x] Summons [x] Complaint

v.

Devon Herschild (DOB: 11/07/1962)

c/o Rest Easy Hotels

1234 Gateway Lane

New Yonkers, Astoria 01298
              Defendant.

The Complainant, being duly sworn, makes complaint to the above-named Court and states that there is probable cause to believe that the Defendant committed the following offense(s):

Count 1	
Charge:	Prohibition of Public Lewdness and Indecency
Statute:	§11.01 – Public Lewdness
Maximum Sentence:	Fine up to $4,000 OR up to 1 year in jail OR both

Count 2	
Charge:	Prohibition of Public Lewdness and Indecency
Statute:	§11.02 – Indecent Exposure
Maximum Sentence:	Fine up to $2,000 OR up to 180 days in jail OR both

Count 3	
Charge:	Prohibition of Obscenity
Statute:	§41.14 – "Contemporary Community Standards" Defined
Maximum Sentence:	None indicated

Statement of Probable Cause

The Defendant is the owner and operator of Rest Easy Hotels, a place of public accommodation licensed to do business in the state of Astoria.

The hotel operates a pay-per-view system through which adult guests can purchase sexually explicit movies that play on television sets provided in their room. On July 14, I, Officer Jennifer Hathaway with the Astoria Police Department, posed as a hotel guest, reserved a room, and used the pay-per-view system to order a sexually explicit movie. The movie ran on the television set in my room, and my account was charged $19.95.

The movie purchased from Rest Easy Hotels was sexually explicit, and qualified as obscene under the above referenced statutes.

Complainant's Name	Complainant's Signature
Officer Jennifer Hathaway City of Astoria Police Department Badge #324	*Jennifer Hathaway*

	Prosecutor's Signature:
Being authorized to prosecute the offenses charged, I approve this complaint. Prosecutor's Name: Kenneth Jones Address: 89 Smithfield Road New Yonkers, Astoria Phone: 888-238-2847 Attorney Registration #: 34879398	*Kenneth Jones*

Finding of Probable Cause

From the above sworn facts, and any supporting affidavits or supplemental sworn testimony, I, the Issuing Officer, have determined that probable cause exists to support Defendant's arrest or other lawful steps to secure an appearance in court, or Defendant's detention, if already in custody, pending further proceedings. Defendant is therefore charged with the above-stated offense.

 Summons

Therefore, you the above-named Defendant, are hereby summoned to appear on the 5th day of August, at 8:30 am, before the above-named court at 1439 Almaeda Avenue, Astoria, to answer this complaint.

This Complaint, duly subscribed and sworn to, is issued by the undersigned Judicial Officer, this 28th of July.

Judicial Officer

Name: Petra Kovicz, Magistrate

Signature: *Petra Kovicz*

Citizens for Family Values

2005 Heaven's Way
New Yonkers, Astoria 01298

Fifty Years of Caring, Commitment and Community

Devon Herschild
Rest Easy Hotels
1234 Gateway Lane
New Yonkers, Astoria 01298

Dear Ms. Herschild:

Citizens for Family Values demands that Rest Easy Hotels cease offering its guests adult-content pay-per-view movies. These sexually explicit films patently offend Astoria's core community values and violate three separate sections of the state code. Those sections are attached to this correspondence.

We understand that Rest Easy Hotels provides unparalleled service to a world-wide clientele. Your advertisements boast that more than 37,000 guests lodged at your downtown facility last year alone. You also hosted the International Governors Conference at the request of Astoria Governor Karine Johnson, and serviced more than 112 dignitaries from across the globe. The five-star reputation associated with your establishment cannot be sustained long-term if Rest Easy continues to pander offensive hard-core entertainment to guests.

As reported in *The Nation Today* newspaper, other national hotel chains, including Comfort Sleep, Merrylodge, and Milton, have wisely discontinued obscene move entertainment. Experts estimate that adult movies generate $5 million in annual revenue for hotel chains, and attribute 50–60% of pay-per-view revenues to adult products. Yet these businesses have chosen to promote the good morals of the community over immoral profits. We hope these developments inspire you to follow their lead.

Sincerely,

Stanli Grover

Stanli Grover
President, Citizens for Family Values

State of Astoria Codified Statutes of 1963, Annotated Prohibition of Public Lewdness and Indecency

§ 11.01 — Public Lewdness

It shall be unlawful in the State of Astoria to:

1. Knowingly engage in one of the following acts in a public place, OR

2. Engage in one of the following acts while reckless as to whether another is present who will be offended or alarmed:

   a. Act of sexual intercourse,

   b. Act of deviate sexual intercourse,

   c. Act of sexual contact, OR

   d. Act of sexual contact with a bird or animal.

Public Lewdness is a Class A misdemeanor.

Class A misdemeanor: Fine up to $4,000 OR up to 1 year in jail OR both.

Historical Reference: 1992 amendment authorized financial penalty as alternative to jail sentence established by Codified Statutes of 1963.

§ 11.02 — Indecent Exposure

It shall be unlawful in the State of Astoria for any individual to:

1. Expose themselves with intent to arouse or gratify the sexual desire of any person, AND

2. The individual exposed knows or has reason to know that another is present who will be offended or alarmed.

This is a Class B misdemeanor.

Class B misdemeanor: Fine up to $2,000 OR up to 180 days in jail OR both.

Historical Reference: 1992 amendment authorized financial penalty as alternative to jail sentence established by Codified Statutes of 1963.

**State of Astoria
Codified Statutes of 1963,
Annotated Prohibition of Obscenity
Contemporary Community Standards**

§ 41.14 — "Contemporary Community Standards" Defined

a. Purpose and Intent

It is the purpose of this statute to define the terms "contemporary standards" and "contemporary community standards" as that term is used as one element of a definition of obscenity;

It is the further purpose of this statute to provide public and private decision-making bodies with a standard or measure by which to determine what constitutes obscenity within the State of Astoria.

b. Standards

Within the State of Astoria, any business which displays, distributes, or engages in commerce involving representations or descriptions of any of the following, whether involving children or adults: ultimate sexual acts, normal or perverted, actual or simulated; and representations or descriptions of masturbatory, excretory functions, and lewd exhibition of the genitals, is determined to be patently offensive to the adults of the State of Astoria, and should be considered by such employees, agents, representatives and governing bodies to "appeal to the prurient interest." All public and private decision-making bodies or individuals shall recognize this as a standard set by the adults of the State of Astoria to be used in determining whether such business is obscene.

Chapter 3

THE FIGHTING WORDS DOCTRINE

INTRODUCTION

The First Amendment may provide a defense if your client is charged with a "disorderly conduct" or "breach of the peace" violation. You will first need to determine the basis for the charge. Was your client arrested on account of disagreeable language, or unruly or disruptive conduct that posed a direct threat to public order and safety? An arrest for jumping a subway turnstile or wielding a knife in public hardly raises a legitimate free speech concern. It may be a closer call, however, when the arrest is based on actual speech.

Speech alone can serve as the basis for a valid arrest when it falls into an unprotected category. The government is free to regulate speech historically subject to proscription at the common law. *See United States v. Stevens*, 130 S. Ct. 1577, 1584 (2010). Such is the case with "fighting words," defined by the Supreme Court as words that by their very utterance inflict injury or tend to provoke an immediate breach of the peace. *Chaplinsky v. New Hampshire*, 315 U.S. 568, 572 (1942). Chaplinsky was a Jehovah's Witness who was convicted for saying to a police officer, " 'You are a God damned racketeer,' and 'a damned Fascist and the whole government of Rochester are Fascists or agents of Fascists.'" The Court concluded that these words were "epithets likely to provoke the average person to retaliation." *Chaplinsky*, 315 U.S. at 574.

Whether an utterance is unprotected fighting words depends on the facts and circumstances of each case. The test is not what a particular addressee thinks, but what people of "common intelligence" think would cause a "reasonable addressee" to fight. Moreover, fighting words must be directed to an intended individual or group or listeners. Consider the use of profanity in *Cohen v. California*, 403 U.S. 15 (1971), where the Supreme Court held that a Vietnam War protestor whose jacket bore the words "fuck the draft" could not be criminally prosecuted for "maliciously and willfully disturbing the peace and quiet." Under the circumstances, Justice Harlan wrote, the expletive was not a "direct personal insult" that was likely to incite a violent response. This was because the jacket's message was neither directed to a specific person nor intended to "provoke[e] a given group to hostile reaction." *Id.* at 20. *See also Texas v. Johnson*, 491 U.S. 397, 409 (1989) (flag burning was not fighting words because "[n]o reasonable onlooker would have regarded Johnson's generalized expression of dissatisfaction with the policies of the Federal Government as a direct personal insult or an invitation to exchange fisticuffs.").

Depending on the circumstances, however, courts might find that profanity is not protected speech. Examples include cases where a defendant cursed at a nude sunbather, displayed a sexually derogatory sign to a motorist, or shouted profanity laced racial slurs to someone waiting at a bus stop. The nature of the inquiry is so fact intensive, however, that disparate results can occur in situations that at first appear quite similar. For instance, a student who gestured a middle finger to school officials was properly convicted of disorderly conduct, whereas a driver who did the same to another motorist was not. *Compare Coggin v. State*, 123 S.W.3d 82 (Tex. App. 2003), *with In re S.J.N.-K*, 647 N.W. 2d 707 (S.D. 2002). Lawyers must examine the surrounding circumstances carefully, including the frequency, volume, and context of the remarks, to make sense of these outcomes.

Some fighting words situations warrant special consideration. First, police officers might be held to a higher standard of restraint than an average citizen on account of their special skills and training. *See Marttila v. City of Lynchburg*, 535 S.E.2d. 693 (Va. Ct. App. 2000). Insults, slurs, and profanity directed to a police officer are therefore less likely to provoke a violent response, and consequently less likely to constitute fighting words, than the same language directed towards an average person. When potential fighting words are directed to a third party, however, the police must make reasonable efforts to control an unruly crowd before arresting the speaker.

Second, even though fighting words are not protected by the First Amendment, content-based measures that prohibit some types of fighting words but not others might trigger strict scrutiny review. Applying that standard, the Supreme Court invalidated an ordinance that punished only fighting words related to race, color, creed, religion or gender, but not fighting words related to other characteristics. *See R.A.V. v. St. Paul*, 505 U.S. 377 (1992). Note the "special virulence" exception, however, which holds that strict scrutiny does not apply when a content-based restriction on a sub-category of speech relates back to the very reason the entire category of speech is unprotected. What does this mean? Well, instead of prohibiting all depictions of obscenity, a state might choose to prohibit only the "most patently offensive" depictions. Strict scrutiny would not apply, as the line between what the state prohibits (the most patently offensive obscenity), and what it allows (less patently offensive obscenity), goes back to the reason why obscenity is not given any First Amendment protection at all — because it is "patently offensive." On the other hand, if the state prohibits only obscene depictions of Republicans (or Democrats), strict scrutiny would apply because political affiliation has nothing to do with the reasons why obscenity is unprotected. In *Virginia v. Black*, 538 U.S. 343 (2003), the Supreme Court applied the special virulence exception to a statute that singled out cross burning as a prohibited form of intimidation, though it ultimately voided the statute on other grounds.

Finally, laws that target bias-motivated speech are treated differently under the First Amendment than laws that address bias-motivated conduct. Compare the ordinance the Court struck down in *R.A.V.*, with the statute it upheld in *Wisconsin v. Mitchell*, 508 U.S. 476 (1993). *Mitchell* involved a sentence enhancement provision that increased the penalty for racially-motivated crimes. The Court rejected the defendant's First Amendment challenge, and distinguished *R.A.V.*, holding that the legislature's "desire to redress the greater individual and societal harm inflicted by bias-inspired conduct provided an adequate explanation for the provision over and above mere disagreement with the offenders' beliefs or biases." *Id.* at 488.

Practice Tip: Students often find it difficult to distinguish between speech in the form of "fighting words" and speech that constitutes a "true threat." A "true threat" is a "statement[] where the speaker means to communicate a serious expression of an intent to commit an unlawful act of violence to a particular individual or group of individuals." *See Virginia v. Black*, 538 U.S. 343, 359 (2003) A hollow threat will suffice, as "[t]he speaker need not actually intend to carry out the threat." *Id.* at 360. Thus, while the fighting words doctrine aims to avoid a violent altercation, the true threats doctrine discourages speech that would place another person in fear, separate and apart from whether the threat would also provoke a fight. Note also that a police officer confronted with a "true threat" will not be held to the same level of heightened restraint expected in a "fighting words" case.

To protect political speech, it is important to distinguish between true threats and political hyperbole. For example, in *Watts v. United States*, 394 U.S. 705 (1969), a young man was convicted for making the following statement at a political rally: "If they ever make me carry a rifle the first man I want to get in my sights is L.B.J." The Court held that this was mere political hyperbole, and not an actual threat, because the statement was conditional ("If they ever make me carry a rifle . . ."), and the words were spoken during a political discussion. *Id.* at 708.

While lower courts have upheld fighting words convictions, the Supreme Court has not upheld such a conviction since *Chaplinsky*. This has caused some authors to question whether a fighting words doctrine still exists.

Furthermore, remember to review the wording and history of the applicable statute to determine whether it is unconstitutionally vague or overbroad. You may need to research whether the statute has been authoritatively construed by a state court, and always be sure that the jury instructions are constitutionally firm. Refer to Chapter 7 for more on the vagueness and overbreadth doctrines.

EXERCISE 3

You are an assistant district attorney assigned to handle the case against Martha Jones, an anti-war activist who was arrested at City International Airport on August 19, while wearing a shirt with the words "Real Patriots Don't Kill Iraqi Children." At the time of the arrest, Jones was standing next to a designated "welcome area" where returning soldiers would reunite with their families. A Transportation Security Administration officer instructed her to change the shirt, cover it up, or leave the area immediately. When Jones refused, the TSA officer moved to escort her out of the area. Jones pulled away from the TSA officer, and told him to "fuck off." Before she left the area, she turned back to the TSA officer and screamed, "I may as well just come back to blow your head off for supporting this fascist war."

You must determine whether the facts are sufficient to prosecute Ms. Jones, and whether the First Amendment operates as a bar to prosecution.

REQUIRED TASKS:

Task 1:   Identify facts that will help you determine whether to prosecute Ms. Jones for breach of the peace.

Task 2:   Assuming the facts are sufficient to support a prosecution, draft a criminal complaint against Ms. Jones that charges her with breaching the peace (the LexisNexis web course contains a form for the complaint that has been started for you).

PRACTICE SKILLS UTILIZED:

Skill 1:   Factual development
Skill 2:   Critical analysis
Skill 3:   Criminal pleading

ESTIMATED TIME FOR COMPLETION: Approximately 1 1/4 hours

LEVEL OF DIFFICULTY (1 TO 5):

Chapter 4

COMMERCIAL SPEECH

INTRODUCTION

The regulation of commercial speech occurs whenever the government creates standards governing the solicitation or advertisement of the products or services of business enterprises. This type of regulation can take many forms. Commercial speech regulations may specify where or when an advertisement or solicitation may occur, how the advertisement or solicitation may be made, or what information may be transmitted in the advertisement or solicitation. Sometimes the government regulations even absolutely ban solicitations or advertisements regarding particular products or services.

Commercial speech cases typically arise when a commercial or business enterprise desires to solicit or advertise in a manner prohibited by the applicable regulations. If the enterprise violates the regulations, the promulgating governmental agency will attempt to enforce sanctions against the enterprise for its conduct, and the entity will assert the First Amendment as a defense. In other cases, the enterprise sues to obtain a declaratory judgment that the First Amendment invalidates the regulations rather than risking penalties for violating the regulations.

Commercial speech issues also arise when an administrative agency reviews advertisements and solicitations before or concurrently with their dissemination to the public. For instance, many state bar organizations regulate attorney advertisements or solicitations, and frequently require the attorney to submit any such advertisements or solicitations to the bar either before or concurrently with their publication to clients.

Although the Supreme Court originally viewed commercial speech as outside the ambit of the First Amendment, its decisions during the 1970s began to offer some constitutional protection, leading to the four-part commercial speech test announced in *Central Hudson Gas & Electric Corp. v. Public Service Commission*, 447 U.S. 557, 566 (1980). First, in order to be protected commercial speech under the First Amendment, the expression must concern lawful activity and not be misleading. The second consideration is whether the government has asserted a substantial governmental interest to regulate the protected commercial speech. The third part analyzes whether the regulation directly advances the governmental interest asserted, and the final part of the *Central Hudson* test requires that the regulation is not more extensive than necessary to serve that interest. *Id.*

Central Hudson employed this test to invalidate a state agency rule that banned promotion of electricity by public utilities. The Court explained that commercial expression deserves First Amendment protection because it serves the economic interests of the speaker, assists consumers, and furthers the societal interest in the dissemination of information in a market economy. Yet the Court refused to accord the same protection to commercial speech enjoyed by other forms of expression. While several Supreme Court Justices have indicated their dissatisfaction with the lesser protection afforded to commercial speech under the *Central Hudson* test, and some of its prongs have generated doctrinal confusion, it remains the applicable standard today.

A preliminary issue that must be addressed before applying the four parts of the *Central Hudson* test is whether the speech at issue is actually commercial speech. While the Supreme Court has indicated that the distinction between commercial and noncommercial speech is a matter of common sense, neither defining nor identifying the scope of commercial speech is always a simple matter. *Central Hudson* described "commercial speech" both as "expression related solely to the economic interests of the speaker and its audience" and as "speech proposing a commercial transaction, which occurs in an area traditionally subject to governmental regulation." 447 U.S. at 561-62. As Justice Stevens pointed out in his concurrence, however, these two descriptions are not identical, with the former appearing broader than the latter. *Id.* at 579-80 (Stevens, J., concurring). Perhaps a better description is that commercial speech entails advertisements or solicitations for profit or another business purpose. In any event, the "sale" of speech (such as paying for a book or a movie) or the economic motivations for speech (such as a labor union picket of an employer) do not transform otherwise fully protected speech into commercial speech subject to the *Central Hudson* standard.

Central Hudson's first prong ensures that the expression at issue is neither misleading nor related to illegal activity. While untruthful or misleading speech generally cannot be proscribed, the different interests in the commercial speech context allow the government to prohibit advertisements or solicitations that are misleading or concern unlawful transactions. Commercial speech, according to the Supreme Court, is a "hardy breed of expression," as the speaker is motivated by economic self-interest. *Central Hudson*, 447 U.S. at 563-64 & n.6. Commercial speakers also have extensive knowledge of the market and their products. Since the primary value to consumers from commercial speech is informational, the government has authority to ban those communications that mislead or concern unlawful activity and thereby fail to provide an informational benefit to consumers. *Id.*

The second part of *Central Hudson* then analyzes whether the governmental interest supporting the regulation is substantial. A variety of asserted governmental interests have been viewed as substantial, including preventing the use of tobacco products by minors, *Lorillard Tobacco Co. v. Reilly*, 533 U.S. 525, 555 (2002); conserving resources, *Central Hudson*, 447 U.S. at 568; ensuring fair utility rates, *id.* at 569; protecting consumers, *Ohralik v. Ohio State Bar Association*, 436 U.S. 447, 460 (1978); and reducing visual blight. *City of Cincinnati v. Discovery Network, Inc.*, 507 U.S. 410, 416 (1993). The government typically does not have difficulty articulating a satisfactory substantial governmental interest for regulating commercial speech — the more difficult questions concern the third and fourth parts of the test.

The third part of *Central Hudson* requires that the regulation directly advance the asserted governmental interest. This necessitates more than speculation or conjecture. While the government does not necessarily have to commission an empirical study, the government must produce evidence that the harms are "real" and the regulation will provide redress "to a material degree." *Lorillard*, 533 U.S. at 555. In some cases the Court has found the required evidence lacking. As an example, advertising bans on professional services do not, according to the Court, directly advance a claimed interest in ethical or professional standards. *Bates v. State Bar of Arizona*, 433 U.S. 350, 378 (1977) (ban on attorney advertising did not directly advance interest in quality of attorney work product); *Virginia Pharmacy Board v. Virginia Citizens Consumer Council*, 425 U.S. 748, 769 (1976) (ban on pharmacy advertising did not advance interest in professional and ethical standards). In other cases the Court has held that a regulation is too remotely related to the asserted governmental interest to satisfy this requirement. *See, e.g.*, *Sorrell v. IMS Health Inc.*, 131 S. Ct. 2653, 2668-70 (2011) (ban solely against the use of pharmacy records by marketers did not advance asserted privacy interests); *Lorillard*, 533 U.S. at 566 (requirement that smokeless tobacco and cigar advertising had to be higher than five feet from the floor did not advance goal to limit youth exposure to advertising); *Central Hudson*, 447 U.S. at 569 (link between ban on promotional advertising and utility rate structure too attenuated to directly advance claimed governmental interest).

The fourth part of the test has been the most challenging, for both the government and even the Court itself. The Court has been inconsistent in the stringency applied in interpreting this prong. Under its recent approach, the regulation does not have to be the least restrictive means, but instead must be reasonably tailored to accomplish its objective. *Lorillard*, 533 U.S. at 556. But such a reasonable fit requires the state to carefully factor the regulation's benefits and the costs imposed by the burden on speech. *Id.* at 561. If the governmental objective could be accomplished as effectively without restricting speech or by restricting less speech, the government cannot satisfy this prong of the analysis. *See, e.g.*, *Thompson v. Western States Medical Center*, 535 U.S. 357, 371-73 (2002) (holding prohibition on advertising compounded drugs more extensive than necessary because the governmental interests could be served without restricting speech); *Lorillard*, 533 U.S. at 562 (holding outdoor advertising regulations on smokeless tobacco and cigars were not carefully calculated to ensure a proper fit when their effect prevented any advertising in 90% of metropolitan areas); *Rubin v. Coors Brewing Co.*, 514 U.S. 476, 491 (1995) (holding ban on displaying alcohol content on beer labels unconstitutional due to other alternatives that could advance the government's interest in a manner less intrusive on speech rights); *Central Hudson*, 447 U.S. at 570 (holding absolute advertising ban suppressed some speech that would not endanger conservation interest supporting the regulation).

The application of this four-part standard to advertising for professional services — including attorney services — has been a frequent issue in the Supreme Court. In *Bates v. State Bar of Arizona*, 433 U.S. 350, 383-84 (1977), the Supreme Court held that attorney advertising is protected under the First Amendment. The Court reasoned that attorney advertising could assist clients in making informed decisions.

Id. at 375. Nevertheless, the Court has upheld those regulations tailored to protect against risks of attorney advertising, such as privacy invasions, undue influence, and overreaching. As a result, the Supreme Court has upheld regulations that prohibit in-person solicitation by an attorney interested in pecuniary gain, *see Ohralik v. Ohio State Bar Association*, 436 U.S. 447, 459-62 (1978), that prohibit written solicitations of a client within thirty days of an accident, *see Florida Bar v. Went For It, Inc.*, 515 U.S. 618, 620-25 (1995), or that compel specified disclosures to ensure that an advertisement is neither false nor misleading in any respect. *Zauderer v. Office of Disciplinary Counsel*, 471 U.S. 626, 652-53 (1985). On the other hand, if the content is not misleading and does not raise the specter of overreaching or invasion of a client's privacy interests, the cases have protected the attorney's right under the First Amendment to advertise. *See, e.g., Shapero v. Kentucky Bar Association*, 486 U.S. 466, 476-80 (1988); *In re R.M.J.*, 455 U.S. 191, 203-07 (1982). But despite these cases, free speech issues concerning attorney advertising continue to arise.

EXERCISE 4

You are a member of the Odin State Bar's Advertising Review Committee. Under Odin's State Bar Rules, the Advertising Review Committee is to review, either before or concurrently with a communication's dissemination, "all written, audio, audio-visual, or digital communication published or transmitted to one or more prospective clients for the purpose of obtaining or that actually results in professional representation." As a member of the committee, you must first view any material brought to your attention and determine whether it is subject to review by your committee and whether it violates the applicable state bar rules. If it violates state bar rules, you then must determine whether the advertisement is nonetheless protected under the First Amendment, employing the *Central Hudson* standard. If you conclude that the rule is constitutional and has been violated, you then must report the matter to the appropriate grievance committee.

PREPARE A MEMORANDUM FOR EACH SET OF MATERIALS TO:

Task 1:   Analyze whether the material is subject to committee review.

Task 2:   Analyze whether the material violates the applicable rules of the State Bar of Odin.

Task 3:   Analyze whether the advertisement may be regulated consistent with the First Amendment.

Task 4:   Identify additional information that you would want to obtain to assist in your analyses.

PRACTICE SKILLS UTILIZED:

Skill 1:   Interpretation of ethical rules and regulations

Skill 2:   Critical statutory and constitutional analysis

Skill 3:   Strategic thinking

ESTIMATED TIME FOR COMPLETION: Approximately 1 hour per set of materials.

LEVEL OF DIFFICULTY (1 TO 5):

PERTINENT REGULATION OF THE STATE BAR OF ODIN:

Rule 13.01 Communications Concerning an Attorney's Services

(A)   A lawyer shall not make or sponsor a false or misleading communication about the qualifications or the services of any lawyer or firm. A communication is false or misleading if it:

    (1)   contains a material misrepresentation of fact or law, or omits a fact necessary to make the statement considered as a whole not materially misleading;

    (2)   contains any reference in a public media advertisement to past successes or results obtained unless

        (i)   the lawyer served as lead counsel or was primarily responsible for the result,

        (ii)   the amount involved was actually received by client,

        (iii)   the reference is accompanied by adequate information regarding the nature of the case or matter and the damages or injuries received by the client, and

        (iv)   if the gross amount received is stated, the attorney's fees and litigation expenses withheld from the amount are stated as well;

    (3)   is likely to create an unjustified expectation about results the lawyer can achieve;

    (4)   compares the lawyer's services with other lawyers' services, unless the comparison can be substantiated by reference to verifiable, objective data;

    (5)   designates one or more specific areas of practice in an advertisement or solicitation unless the lawyer is competent to handle legal matters in such an area of practice;

    (6)   uses an actor or model to portray a client of the lawyer or law firm;

    (7)   portrays the lawyer with characteristics unrelated to legal competence;

    (8)   uses a nickname, moniker, motto, or trade name that implies an ability to obtain results; or

    (9)   depicts a courthouse or a courtroom to indicate the lawyer's legal prowess.

(B)   A lawyer shall not accept or continue employment in a matter when that employment was procured by conduct prohibited by this rule. The failure of an attorney to abide by this rule is subject to appropriate discipline.

The following four sets of materials have been brought to the Committee's attention for analysis:

#1 — Transcript of Radio Advertisement

When you need a lawyer, there's only one choice — Max "The Pit Bull" Jones. I'm the toughest lawyer in town [dogs growling in the background]. I can obtain money for you even when other lawyers cannot. Listen to what my clients have to say about me:

> Voice #1: I went to three other lawyers before I went to see the Pit Bull, but they were all wimps. Max Jones scared the other side into settling my car accident claim for $150,000. Thanks Max "The Pit Bull" Jones!

> Voice #2: If you want to get money, there's only one lawyer to see — the Pit Bull. He's tough, he's mean, and he's scary as hell to the other side. I got $300,000 for my claim, even though my sober friends told me the accident was my fault. Thanks Max "The Pit Bull" Jones!

I could go on and on with similar stories. I've gotten those idiotic insurance companies to pay over $100 million to me and my clients. [Dogs start growling in the background again]. So when you need a lawyer, don't forget who to call — Max "The Pit Bull" Jones — 1-800-PIT-BULL. That number again is 1-800-PIT-BULL. [Growling fades out].

#2 — Transcript of Radio Interview

NEWS ANCHOR: We have breaking news from the local county courthouse. Over a year ago, a deadly explosion at the XYZ Manufacturing Plant killed 50 workers and injured hundreds of other workers and local residents. The jury in one of the many lawsuits that was filed as a result has just reached a verdict, awarding $10 million to the family of one of the workers, Zip Tucker, who was killed in the explosion. Joining me live for a discussion about this jury verdict is Wright Justice, a local personal injury attorney who is representing a number of the other victims of this tragedy. Mr. Justice, why is this verdict significant?

MR. JUSTICE: Primarily because the jury rejected XYZ's defense that the explosion was merely an unavoidable accident for which it should not be held responsible. Instead, the jury, relying on the company's long history of safety violations, concluded that not only was the company responsible for the damages caused to Mr. Tucker, but that it also had to pay punitive or exemplary damages because its conduct was so outrageous that punishment was warranted.

NEWS ANCHOR: But isn't the amount of the damages awarded here equally outrageous? Is this a case of a jury run amok?

MR. JUSTICE: Actually, I think the jury award was, if anything, too low. In my past experiences handling death cases arising from similar types of plant catastrophes, I've usually been able to obtain higher jury awards, especially in cases where the jury awards punitive damages. The jury mostly awarded the Tucker family economic damages for his future loss income, and awarded relatively modest punitive damages and mental anguish damages. I think a stronger case could have been easily made that more punitive and mental anguish damages should have been awarded, especially considering the net worth and reprehensible conduct of XYZ. I'm certainly going to seek higher damage awards in my cases.

NEWS ANCHOR: Well, that brings up a good point. How will this jury award impact other pending claims against XYZ?

MR. JUSTICE: I'm hopeful that this will induce XYZ to start trying to negotiate a reasonable settlement. And what I think a reasonable settlement will be in my cases is certainly going to be influenced by the $10 million jury award in Mr. Tucker's case and my belief that I could have even obtained a higher jury award.

NEWS ANCHOR: Anything else of significance from today's events?

MR. JUSTICE: It does illustrate the need to obtain competent legal representation in these cases. If you're a victim of this explosion who hasn't yet visited with a lawyer about your claim, please do so soon — the statute of limitations for your claims will soon expire, so you need to get a lawyer now. It's best to get a law firm with experience in these types of claims.

NEWS ANCHOR: Thanks for joining us today, Mr. Justice.

MR. JUSTICE: It was my pleasure.

NEWS ANCHOR: That was Wright Justice, with the local law firm of Justice & Justice. Now in other news stories today. . . .

#3 — See LexisNexis Web Course for Materials

#4 — See LexisNexis Web Course for Materials

Chapter 5

LIBEL, DEFAMATION, AND OTHER TORTS

INTRODUCTION

As children, we were told, "Sticks and stones may break my bones, but words will never hurt me." As adults, we realize that saying is more wish than reality. And as lawyers, we know that the common law of torts recognizes that words can legally "hurt" us. A long line of Supreme Court cases struggles to draw the boundary between tort liability for harmful words and First Amendment protection of free speech.

The Court drew an important part of the boundary in the canonical case *New York Times v. Sullivan*, 376 U.S. 254 (1964). The New York Times had published a political advertisement that accused Alabama law enforcement officials of racially-motivated misconduct. A law enforcement official sued for libel per se under state common law, which made a publisher liable for statements of fact tending to injure the reputation of a public official regardless of proof of actual damages. The publisher could avoid liability only by proving that the statements were true.

The Court held that Alabama's no fault liability scheme for false statements about public officials on matters of public concern violated the First Amendment. In such cases, a publisher or speaker can only be liable for false statements of fact made with "actual malice," which means "with knowledge that it was false or with reckless disregard of whether it was false or not." *Id.* at 279-80. The public official bears the burden of pleading and proving both that the statements were false, and that they were made with actual malice. Further, a public official can only recover actual damages.

Since *Sullivan*, the Court has extended the actual malice rule to libel and defamation claims against public figures. The Court has explained that a public figure can be either general or limited. A general public figure is someone with general fame or notoriety, such as a former president or a famous celebrity. *Gertz v. Robert Welch, Inc.*, 418 U.S. 323, 351 (1974) ("In some instances an individual may achieve such pervasive fame or notoriety that he becomes a public figure for all purposes and in all contexts."). The actual malice standard will apply to any libel or defamation claim by a general public figure. A limited public figure is someone whose fame or notoriety is tied to a specific subject or event. *Id.* ("an individual voluntarily injects himself or is drawn into a particular public controversy and thereby becomes a public figure for a limited range of issues"). To be a limited public figure, though, a person must voluntarily make use of or seek media attention. Receipt of federal research grant funding, *Hutchinson v. Proxmire*, 443 U.S. 111, 135-36 (1979), representation of a notorious client, *Gertz*, 418 U.S. at 351, and filing of a divorce proceeding, *Time, Inc.*

v. Firestone, 424 U.S. 448, 454-55 (1976), are not sufficient to make a person a limited public figure.

The Court has given states more leeway to impose liability when a private figure sues for defamation or libel for statements on a matter of public concern. In *Gertz*, the Court held that, "so long as they do not impose liability without fault, the States may define for themselves the appropriate standard of liability for a publisher or broadcaster of defamatory falsehood injurious to a private individual." 418 U.S. at 347. In other words, the publisher or speaker may be liable for false statements made with negligence or a higher degree of fault. The Court has not decided whether a state can impose liability without fault for libel or defamation of a private figure on a matter of private concern. *Cf. Dun & Bradstreet, Inc. v. Greenmoss Builders, Inc.*, 472 U.S. 749, 760-61 (1985) (opinion of Powell, J.) (permitting presumed and punitive damages without a showing of actual malice in defamation action by private figure on a matter of private concern).

In *Masson v. New Yorker Magazine, Inc.*, 501 U.S. 496 (1991), the Court explained how the actual malice standard applies to a journalist's alteration of quotations from a public figure. A Harvard professor sued the New Yorker Magazine for defamation for quotes attributed to him that the reporter conceded had been altered. The Court explained that "a deliberate alteration of the words uttered by a plaintiff [can support civil liability only if] the alteration results in a material change in the meaning conveyed by the statement." *Id.* at 517. So, authors will not be liable for alterations that merely improve style or facilitate understanding (e.g., correcting grammar), but that do not materially change the speaker's meaning.

With the Court's tight restrictions on defamation and libel claims, plaintiffs have turned to other torts when suing over hurtful words. In *Hustler Magazine, Inc. v. Falwell*, 485 U.S. 46 (1988), Reverend Jerry Falwell tried to avoid the actual malice rule by suing Hustler magazine for the tort of intentional infliction of emotional distress, which imposes liability on outrageous conduct intended to cause severe emotional harm. Hustler magazine had published a parody advertisement that described Falwell engaging in incest with his mother. Because the advertisement was an obvious parody, and so no reader would see it as stating facts, Falwell could not make a defamation claim under *Sullivan*. The Court held that Falwell could not avoid *Sullivan* simply by pleading intentional infliction of emotional distress. Discussion of public figures is often outrageous and calculated to cause some emotional distress or discomfort, and so tort liability on that basis would unduly chill public debate. *Id.* at 56 ("public figures and public officials may not recover for the tort of intentional infliction of emotional distress by reason of publications such as the one here at issue without showing in addition that the publication contains a false statement of fact which was made with 'actual malice'"). *See also Snyder v. Phelps*, 131 S. Ct. 1207, 1220 (2011) (overturning liability for intentional infliction of emotional distress when a speaker protested a military funeral and "addressed matters of public import on public property, in a peaceful manner, in full compliance with the guidance of local officials").

Practice Tip: For libel or defamation claims on matters of public concern, the Court has held that a speaker is only liable for false statements of fact, and not statements of opinion that do not contain provably false factual connotations:

[A] statement on matters of public concern must be provable as false before there can be liability under state defamation law, at least in situations, like the present, where a media defendant is involved. Thus, unlike the statement, "In my opinion Mayor Jones is a liar," the statement, "In my opinion Mayor Jones shows his abysmal ignorance by accepting the teachings of Marx and Lenin," would not be actionable. [A] statement of opinion relating to matters of public concern which does not contain a provably false factual connotation will receive full constitutional protection.

Milkovich, 497 U.S. at 19-20.

EXERCISE 5

Your law firm represents Scoopers Weekly, a supermarket tabloid focusing on celebrity gossip, sex, and scandal. Scoopers has a reputation for pursuing stories that most mainstream press outlets will ignore. One way it generates such stories is by paying sources for tips, a practice not condoned by other media outlets. Scoopers has been sued for libel a number of times in the past, sometimes successfully. It wants to avoid additional defamation judgments, but it recognizes that tawdry headlines and juicy stories sell.

You have just been asked to review a story Scoopers is planning on publishing in its next issue. The target of the story, Ima Goode, has threatened through her agent to sue for libel if any defamatory falsehoods are included in the published version of the story. Scoopers has provided your firm the draft story and the written notes from the reporter on his interviews and research that led to the draft. Your firm has asked you to review the draft for any content that a court might hold to be defamatory, to suggest how to revise the planned story to prevent a defamation judgment, and to consider any additional inquiries that should be made before the story is printed.

10/15 DRAFT STORY

PROPOSED HEADLINE: Ima Goode Caught in Drug and Prostitution Scandal

On television, eighteen year-old actress Ima Goode, star of the wholesome family television show "Goode Family," is reverent, loyal, and kind. The star has also attempted to portray herself to the public in a similar manner. She still lives with her parents in a small community outside of San Diego. She avoids the night club scene frequented by so many other young stars. When interviewed, she is humble, respectful, and pious. But her carefully projected persona is a lie.

The FBI is investigating her connection to a drug and prostitution ring centered in San Diego. FBI agents interviewed Ms. Goode at her home on October 13, although Ms. Goode refused to be interviewed without her attorneys being present to assist her with the interview. Reports indicate that the criminal syndicate she's connected to smuggles large quantities of drugs and human trafficking victims over the southern California border each year. According to the United States Attorney, this is the "largest and most inhumane criminal enterprise operating in San Diego County."

The stories of these human trafficking victims are heart-wrenching. Young Anna was forcibly taken from her home by a Mexican drug cartel and then sold to the criminal syndicate and forced into a life of prostitution and dope selling. And hundreds of other victims have similar stories.

While no charges have yet to be filed against Ms. Goode, the impact on her career will likely be devastating. Her portrayal of a wholesome teenager on television cannot be reconciled with her connection to a criminal enterprise that victimizes and abuses hundreds of teenagers from less fortunate backgrounds. According to one insider, "Her public persona is so goody two-shoes, but this revelation should set the record straight as to the real Ima Goode, who's not so good."

NOTES FROM THE DESK OF TONY "SCOOP" JONES

10-13 Received call from Don Bill. Claims to be a neighbor of Ima Goode. Wanted to know payment for tip on story. I told him it depended on the tip. He said a lot of action in front of the Goode house today - various groups of people dressed in suits came to her place. He was outside when one of the groups came to the door of her home, and he overheard them say they were with the FBI. I told him I would check it out and get back to him.

Placed call into source at San Diego Police Department. He said FBI was engaged in a joint investigation with the department on a major narcotics and human trafficking criminal syndicate operating in San Diego. He supposes the FBI may have questioned Goode about that investigation. Told me federal US Atty's office would hold news conference soon about the syndicate.

10-14 Attended morning news conference. US Attorney said: "We have secured indictments against the organizers of the largest and most inhumane criminal enterprise operating in San Diego County. This enterprise has smuggled large quantities of drugs into the US from Mexico. Worst, it is engaged in human trafficking atrocities. Hundreds of teenagers have been taken from their homes and forced into a life of prostitution and drug distribution." In response to question about Goode, said that Goode was questioned because her personal cell phone number was in the contacts list of one of the members of the syndicate who was arrested. He said they had dated a couple of times in high school before she became a star, and he still called her from time to time. FBI went to her house to confirm, and she cooperated fully. Said she knew nothing of his criminal activities, although she admitted to talking to him on occasion and dating him a couple of times a few years earlier.

10-15 Calls to various Hollywood sources. Quote from T.X.: "Ima Goode's public persona is so goody two-shoes, but not everyone in Hollywood likes her, as they think the real Ima Goode can't be that good. This revelation of her connection to a criminal enterprise should set the record straight."

Also called Goode's agent. Told that the story should accurately portray that Goode only was acquainted with one person involved in the syndicate and she had no knowledge of his criminal activities or Goode would sue. Did confirm that FBI agents came to her house and asked questions.

Wrote story, but after suit threats, thought lawyers should get involved. Editor agreed.

REQUIRED TASKS:

Task 1:   Review the draft story for any content that could subject
                 Scoopers Weekly to liability for defamation under applicable First
                 Amendment standards.

Task 2:   Revise the draft story to make it wholly protected under
                 applicable First Amendment standards (the LexisNexis Web
                 Course contains an editable version of the draft story).

Task 3:   Identify any additional inquiries that should be made before the
                 story is printed.

PRACTICE SKILLS UTILIZED:

Skill 1:   Legal analysis
Skill 2:   Revising and editing
Skill 3:   Strategic thinking

ESTIMATED TIME FOR COMPLETION: Approximately 1 hour

LEVEL OF DIFFICULTY (1 TO 5):

Chapter 6

TIME, PLACE, AND MANNER RESTRICTIONS

INTRODUCTION

Much of what that takes place in law school might be described as "passive learning." Your primary task as a law student is to discern the rule of law as announced in appellate cases and understand the reasoning that leads to a particular outcome. Surely this is no small task, particularly when First Amendment cases are concerned, but it differs markedly from tasks that require active reasoning.

Active reasoning requires that you assess the validity of the information you are given based on prior knowledge. For example, passive learning was involved when you read *Clark v. Community for Creative Non-Violence*, 468 U.S. 288 (1984) and *Ward v. Rock Against Racism*, 491 U.S. 781 (1989), to discern the applicable test in a time, place, or manner case. Conversely, active reasoning occurs when you apply that test to a particular fact pattern. It also occurs when you are asked on an exam whether a hypothetical court applied the appropriate rule of law under the circumstances. Rather than accept the validity of the court's judgment, you critically analyze whether the judgment is consistent with established constitutional standards.

As a lawyer, you will continue to engage in passive learning whenever you research the applicable law that applies to your client's case. Other tasks require a higher level of engagement. Opinion drafting and appellate advocacy are two such examples.

If you work as a judicial extern during law school, or as a judicial clerk following law school, you will be asked to review draft opinions, and may even be asked to compose the first draft of an opinion that ultimately will be published under your judge's name. In doing so, your job is to minimize the risk that your judge's opinion will be overturned on appeal. You must therefore learn to spot errors or misstatements of law in written material before they are incorporated into a final opinion.

The same critical inquiry is required when a practicing lawyer seeks to appeal an adverse judgment. Effective appellate advocacy requires not only that you understand the basis for the trial court's conclusion, but that you identify points of law the trial court misapplied. The cases in your text book reached the appellate level precisely because a skillful lawyer identified fatal errors in the lower court's judgment.

Think of the following time, place, and manner problem as an exercise in active reasoning. It requires that you understand the relevant constitutional doctrine and that you affirmatively engage that knowledge to determine whether and how a draft judicial opinion should be revised.

A content-neutral time, place, or manner regulation is constitutional if it is narrowly tailored to serve a substantial government interest that is unrelated to the suppression of expression, and leaves open ample alternative channels for communication. Remember that here, the narrow tailoring inquiry is significantly less demanding than it is under a content-based strict scrutiny case. For example, in *Clark*, the Court upheld a National Park Service regulation that prohibited overnight camping in certain national parks. *Clark* involved demonstrators who wanted to hold a "24-hour vigil" on the National Mall to raise awareness of homelessness. As part of the demonstration, the organizers planned a symbolic tent village where demonstrators could take shelter and sleep when needed. Based on the regulation, however, the Park Service prohibited sleeping in the symbolic tents. The Court concluded that the anti-camping regulation was a permissible time, place, and manner restriction that was not aimed at preventing speech:

> [T]he regulation narrowly focuses on the Government's substantial interest in maintaining the parks in the heart of our Capital in an attractive and intact condition, readily available to the millions of people who wish to see and enjoy them by their presence. To permit camping — using these areas as living accommodations — would be totally inimical to these purposes, as would be readily understood by those who have frequented the National Parks across the country and observed the unfortunate consequences of the activities of those who refuse to confine their camping to designated areas.

468 U.S. at 296. The Court specifically rejected the argument that the regulation was unconstitutional because the Park Service could have adopted a less speech-restrictive alternative to protect the parks, such as limiting "the size, duration, or frequency of demonstrations." *Id.* at 299. The Court would not question the government's determination that the content-neutral sleeping ban was needed to protect the national parks. *Id.*

Ward applied the same analysis to a city regulation that required performers at an outdoor city venue to use sound amplification equipment and personnel provided by the city. The regulation was intended to limit sound volume to protect the peace and quiet of neighboring residential areas. The Court upheld the city regulation as a content-neutral time, place, and manner regulation. The Court explained that a narrowly-tailored regulation need not be the least speech-restrictive alternative:

> Lest any confusion on the point remain, we reaffirm today that a regulation of the time, place, or manner of protected speech must be narrowly tailored to serve the government's legitimate, content-neutral interests but that it need not be the least restrictive or least intrusive means of doing so. Rather, the requirement of narrow tailoring is satisfied "so long as the . . . regulation promotes a substantial government interest that would be achieved less effectively absent the regulation." To be sure, this standard does not mean that a time, place, or manner regulation may burden substantially more speech than is necessary to further the government's legitimate interests. Government may not regulate expression in such a manner that a substantial portion of the burden on speech does not serve to advance its goals. So long as the means chosen are not substantially broader than necessary to achieve the

government's interest, however, the regulation will not be invalid simply because a court concludes that the government's interest could be adequately served by some less-speech-restrictive alternative.

491 U.S. at 798-800.

Practice Tip: Be sure you understand the difference between a time, place, and manner analysis under *Clark* and *Ward*, and an analysis of expressive conduct under *United States v. O'Brien*, 391 U.S. 367 (1968), particularly as it relates to regulations on the "manner" of speech. Note that sometimes, as in *Clark*, the Court may apply both tests to the same expressive conduct.

EXERCISE 6

You are an extern working for a judge who has asked you to review a draft opinion she wrote in a case involving a First Amendment challenge to a security perimeter that surrounds the San Francisco Convention Center. Your job is to identify any problems with the opinion that might provide a basis for appeal.

REQUIRED TASKS:

Task 1:   Identify erroneous statements of law or unclear passages in the draft opinion.

Task 2:   Revise the opinion to correct any misstatements of law, and include appropriate citations to cases (the LexisNexis Web Course contains a version of the opinion that you can revise).

PRACTICE SKILLS UTILIZED:

Skill 1:   Legal analysis
Skill 2:   Opinion drafting

ESTIMATED TIME FOR COMPLETION: Approximately 45 minutes

LEVEL OF DIFFICULTY (1 TO 5):

DRAFT OPINION — NOT APPROVED FOR PUBLICATION

CITY OF SAN FRANCISCO v. AMERICAN FREE SPEECH UNION, ET AL.
United States District Court
Northern District of California

ROBERTA J. KROGER, DISTRICT JUDGE.

This case involves a First Amendment challenge to a security perimeter surrounding a new Convention Center in San Francisco, California. The controversy arises from the following facts.

I. Facts

The San Francisco Convention Center is scheduled to open in three weeks with its first official event, the annual California Chili Cook-Off. Over the next 12 months, a number of conventions, meetings, concerts, political rallies and entertainment events are scheduled to take place at the Convention Center.

The Convention Center grounds include several large parking lots adjacent to four small buildings, and a large, circular enclosed building used as the main exhibit hall. The hall has a capacity to hold up to 20,000 people, and another five to eight thousand people can assemble on the grounds outside.

Cage Free is a non-profit group that seeks to draw public attention to major food production companies that fail to comply with federal regulations regarding the ethical treatment of animals. The group plans to hold a rally at the Chili Cook-Off to protest several such companies whose products will be featured there. Cage Free asserts that a security perimeter established on the grounds of the Convention Center unconstitutionally interferes with its right of free speech by restricting access to a public forum.

Following a review of security measures undertaken in Boston, Chicago, and New York, the San Francisco City Council voted to establish a designated security perimeter at all Convention Center events. The relevant municipal code states that the perimeter is meant "to provide security at Convention Center events by deterring attacks involving explosives and weapons."

The security perimeter includes a "Public Demonstration Zone" where Cage Free can assemble for purposes of holding a rally or engaging in public protest. The Zone is located on a sidewalk 200 feet from one of four entrances to the Convention Center. Though individuals who seek to access the Convention Center must pass through a security screening, no such screening is required of persons inside the Zone. The Zone is enclosed by two rings of concrete barriers set eight feet apart that aid in the apprehension of protestors who evade the inner barrier. No obstructions blocks the area between the sidewalk and the edge of the Zone, so anyone wishing to do so could walk to the outer concrete barrier and be within eight feet of the demonstrators inside.

II. Analysis

Neither Congress nor the states may make a law "abridging the freedom of speech . . . or the right of the people peaceably to assemble. . . ." But First Amendment rights are not absolute, and the government may impose reasonable restrictions on the time, place, and manner of speech in a public forum. This type of restriction is constitutional as long as: (1) it is justified without regard to the content of the speech; (2) it is narrowly tailored to serve a significant government interest; and (3) ample alternative channels for communication of the desired message remain available. Where a First Amendment violation is alleged, the complaining party must prove that the restrictions affect protected expression in a traditional public forum and do not meet the three elements of the time, place, and manner test.

Time, place, or manner restrictions must be narrowly tailored to serve a significant governmental interest. The court finds that preventing the likelihood of a security breach at the San Francisco Convention Center warrants some kind of government action, and therefore proceeds to the narrow tailoring analysis.

A government restriction on speech is narrowly tailored if there are "no alternative means that would more precisely and narrowly" meet the government's objective. *U.S. v. O'Brien*, 391 U.S. 367, 381 (1968). In other words, if the regulation burdens more speech than necessary to further the significant governmental interest, it impermissibly infringes upon First Amendment rights.

Moreover, broad, generic recitals of "security concerns" may not be used to automatically validate burdens on First Amendment rights. Rather, the government must demonstrate that particular measures are needed to protect against foreseeable harms caused by the party denied access a public forum. *Ward v. Rock Against Racism*, 491 U.S. 781, 801 (1989). The regulation's effectiveness is not judged by considering all the hypothetical groups that might some day use the facility. *Clark v. Community for Creative Non-Violence*, 468 U.S. 288, 296–97 (1984).

To justify the security plan, the City points specifically to concerns about attacks by weapons and explosive devices. While these are indeed grave concerns, the security plan affects more speech than necessary to further these interests. Under the proposed security plan, individuals who wish to enter the Zone are not subject to security screening; only individuals who enter the Convention Center are screened. The City could require all demonstrators or protestors to undergo a rigorous security screening before entering the Zone; thereby allowing an opportunity to temporarily confiscate non-speech-related items. The Zone could then be moved closer to the Convention Center and to the participants' path.

Moreover, as situated, the Zone significantly interferes with Cage Free's ability to reach its intended audience. While individuals who enter through the main entry gate come within view and earshot of protesters stationed in the Zone, alternative points of entry are far from the designated protest vicinity. The resulting burden on Cage Free's ability to reach a desired audience works a direct and substantial harm to their First Amendment interests in a way that has not been tolerated in similar cases. See *Ward v. Rock Against Racism*, 491 U.S. 781, 802–03 (1989).

III. Conclusion

The security plan is not narrowly tailored to advance the important governmental interests at play in this case. The restricted protest Zone burdens more speech than is necessary in a manner that fails the second prong of the time, place, and manner standard of review. As such, a permanent injunction is granted against the City and the security plan must be revised so as not to impermissibly infringe upon fundamental First Amendment rights.

Chapter 7

VAGUENESS AND OVERBREADTH

INTRODUCTION

In order for the expressive rights to have the breathing space necessary to adequately advance their purposes, the Supreme Court has created several procedural protections that supplement the substantive contours of protected First Amendment freedoms. One procedural protection is that the issue of whether particular speech falls within the ambit of the First Amendment is typically viewed as a question of law rather than of fact, allowing for de novo judicial review. Two other important procedural protections are the availability of "overbreadth" and "vagueness" challenges to regulations burdening expression.

Overbreadth and vagueness are related but distinct challenges that provide additional avenues to invalidate a law or administrative sanction infringing on expressive rights. Even if the law or sanction could be applied to your client's actual or contemplated expressive activities under substantive First Amendment standards, these doctrines provide a potential for invalidating a regulation that has a chilling effect on expressive rights. Both doctrines may be raised either as a defense to the enforcement of a criminal or administrative sanction or as a basis for a pre-enforcement challenge to a statute or other regulation.

Overbreadth focuses on the scope and precision of the challenged regulation, while vagueness relates to the clarity of the regulation. An overbroad law regulates much more speech than allowed under substantive standards, whereas a vague statute does not provide fair notice of its scope. A regulation that is overbroad or vague cannot be applied, unless a court with appropriate jurisdiction limits or otherwise construes the statute to apply in a constitutional manner.

A statute is unconstitutionally overbroad when it prohibits substantially more speech than is constitutionally permissible. *Board of Airport Commissioners of Los Angeles v. Jews for Jesus. Inc.*, 482 U.S. 569, 573-75 (1987). While there is no precise formula for measuring when a statute is substantially overbroad (as opposed to marginally or merely somewhat overbroad), the analysis entails a comparison between the breadth of the challenged statute and the quantity of speech the government could permissibly regulate. The first step, then, is to determine the scope of the statute at issue. *See United States v. Williams*, 553 U.S. 285, 293 (2008). The second step evaluates whether such a scope infringes upon a substantial amount of protected expression under First Amendment doctrine. *Id.* at 297. If the statute does so, it is subject to invalidation for overbreadth. It is not enough, though, for the unconstitutional applications of the statute to amount to a "tiny fraction" of the statute's reach, *New York v. Ferber*, 458 U.S. 747, 773 (1982) — instead, the statute must be "susceptible of regular application to protected expression." *City of Houston v. Hill*, 482 U.S. 451, 466-67 (1987). As an illustration, evaluating whether a prohibition against "annoying or insulting comments directed to a sidewalk pedestrian" is unconstitutionally overbroad depends on how far the statute reaches beyond a permissible public forum restriction. Under a textual analysis, this prohibition appears very broad, reaching not only those "annoying or insulting comments" that fall within unprotected speech categories such as fighting words, but also other "annoying or insulting" comments that constitute protected First Amendment expression. Such a breadth would infringe upon a substantial amount of protected expression and would be unconstitutionally overbroad in the absence of a limiting construction.

Because of concerns that the threat of enforcement of an overbroad law may chill constitutionally protected speech of individuals who are hesitant to risk prosecution, an overbreadth challenge may be made even by someone whose conduct is within the constitutionally valid scope of the regulation. *See Gooding v. Wilson*, 405 U.S. 518, 521-22 (1972). Such application of the overbreadth doctrine is "manifestly, strong medicine," as it bars the statute from being enforced against any defendant, even one whose speech or conduct is criminally proscribable. *Broadrick v. Oklahoma*, 413 U.S. 601, 615 (1973). In practice, the doctrine allows a defendant who engages in unprotected fighting words to challenge the enforcement of a broadly written "disorderly conduct" statute on the theory that other persons will refrain from engaging in protected speech for fear of being prosecuted themselves. *Cf. Gooding*, 405 U.S. at 521-28., The doctrine effectively modifies constitutional standing requirements that typically bar an individual from asserting a claim on behalf of another person not before the court. The supporting rationale is that permitting the defendant's unprotected speech to go unpunished is considered a less significant harm than the chilling effect a substantially overbroad statute will have on protected speech.

The other procedural doctrine, vagueness, emanates from the due process guarantee and applies when a statute fails to meet a threshold standard of notice and definiteness. Although complete precision in language is perhaps an unattainable goal, the premise is that an individual must have fair notice as to what is prohibited before being subject to punishment for noncompliance. Due process dictates that a statute is vague if persons "of average intelligence must necessarily guess at its meaning and differ as to its application." *Connally v. General Construction Co.*, 269 U.S. 385, 391 (1926). Under this standard, an ordinance that prohibits individuals from assembling on a sidewalk and conducting themselves "in a manner annoying to persons walking by" is unconstitutionally vague because it does not provide an ascertainable standard for determining what type of proscribable conduct is "annoying." *See Coates v. City of Cincinnati*, 402 U.S. 611, 614-15 (1971).

Fair notice is especially important in the free speech context as such uncertainty may stifle expression and risk selective prosecution against those with unpopular views. *Grayned v. City of Rockford*, 408 U.S. 104, 108-09 (1972). Particular vigilance is warranted when a statute prohibits speech because individuals may hesitate to engage in constitutionally protected expression for fear of violating an indecipherable law. Drafting precision also provides guidance to law enforcement officers and guards against the risk that a statute will be selectively enforced against an unpopular speaker. As a result, a statute will be invalidated as unconstitutionally vague if it "fails to provide a person of ordinary intelligence fair notice of what is prohibited, or is so standardless that it authorizes or encourages seriously discriminatory enforcement." *Williams*, 553 U.S. at 304.

Frequently, vagueness and overbreadth claims overlap, but they are conceptually distinct. As an example, a law barring "any verbal expression or speech" at a particular location could be understood by persons of common intelligence such that it would not be subject to a vagueness challenge, although certainly such a law would be unconstitutionally overbroad. *Cf. Jews for Jesus*, 482 U.S. at 574-75. On the other hand, a regulation with an appropriate scope, such as "all expressive activities not protected by the First Amendment are prohibited," would not be overbroad, even though such a regulation would be vague because persons of common intelligence would not be able to ascertain whether their expression was prohibited.

Another difference between these two doctrines is that a vagueness challenge under recent precedent may not be made by a plaintiff if the application of the statute is only vague with respect to the speech and actions of others. In other words, the statute must be vague with respect to expressive activities the plaintiff has either undertaken or, in pre-enforcement challenges, desires to undertake. *See Holder v. Humanitarian Law Project*, 130 S. Ct. 2705, 2718-19 (2010). In contrast, an overbreadth challenge can be made even in circumstances when the statute's only infirmity is that it regularly applies to the protected speech of others.

> ***Practice Tip:*** The text of the statute alone is not controlling in an overbreadth or vagueness challenge if a court of competent jurisdiction has limited or otherwise construed the statute to apply in a constitutional manner. Such a construction of a state statute in a case pending in federal court may be obtained through certification if the state allows federal courts to certify questions to its state supreme court.

> Another factor to keep in mind is whether the statute contains a "severability clause" that signals the lawmakers' intent that part of a statute is to remain in effect if any other part is found unconstitutional. This is one way of preserving the integrity of a broad statutory scheme when one particular aspect of the scheme is rendered invalid for either vagueness or overbreadth.

EXERCISE 7

You are a criminal defense attorney in Massachusetts whose clients are charged with having violated various state code provisions and municipal ordinances. In addition to defending each case on the merits, you also plan to assert an overbreadth or vagueness challenge where appropriate.

The information below indicates the procedural posture of each client's case, the relevant statute or ordinance, and the preliminary results of research you have conducted thus far. Indicate in each circumstance whether an overbreadth or vagueness challenge is likely to succeed.

REQUIRED TASKS:

Task 1:   Determine whether the law in question is substantially overbroad or impermissibly vague.

Task 2:   Revise the statute or ordinance so that it is more likely to withstand a constitutional attack (the LexisNexis Web Course contains an editable version of each statute or ordinance).

PRACTICE SKILL UTILIZED:

Skill 1:   Critical analysis
Skill 2:   Legislative drafting

ESTIMATED TIME FOR COMPLETION: Approximately 45 minutes

LEVEL OF DIFFICULTY (1 TO 5):

Case 1:

Your client is charged with violating an ordinance that bans "three or more persons from assembling on a sidewalk in a manner intended to annoy others." Your client was standing on a sidewalk with three other friends when they flipped off a police officer who was driving on the other side of the road. The officer arrested all four of them and charges were brought in state court.

You determine that:

- The ordinance is contained in a criminal code subchapter dealing with criminal activities by gang members and is intended to discourage illegal gang activity.

- The ordinance has not yet been interpreted by a Massachusetts state court.

- *Coates v. City of Cincinnati*, 402 U.S. 611 (1971), invalidated a similar statute on vagueness grounds because it provided no ascertainable standard of conduct by which an average person could determine what was prohibited.

Could you successfully assert a vagueness challenge?

Could you successfully assert an overbreadth challenge?

Case 2:

Your client is charged with violating a state statute that prohibits "the sale or distribution of any material that is obscene." Your client had sold a movie containing graphic depictions of bestiality to an undercover police officer. Charges are pending in state court.

You determine that:

- The statute has not been narrowed by any construction of the state supreme court.

- *Board of Airport Commissioners of Los Angeles v. Jews for Jesus, Inc.*, 482 U.S. 569 (1987), invalidated a statute that prohibited "all First Amendment activities" in the Los Angeles airport as substantially overbroad.

Can you successfully assert a vagueness challenge?

Can you successfully assert an overbreadth challenge?

Case 3:

A city ordinance prohibits juveniles from "perusing" city streets between the hours of 7:00 a.m. and 3:00 p.m. "Perusing" is defined as "placing one's self on a city street without a clear objective." Your client is arrested and charged with violating the ordinance for skipping some of her morning classes to wander around the streets close to her school as she contemplated a test she had that afternoon.

Before trial, you discover that:

- The ordinance is intended to curb juvenile truancy and loitering.

- In a previous case, the Massachusetts Supreme Court concluded that the ordinance was unconstitutionally vague because it gave police officers absolute discretion to determine what activities constitute "perusing."

- You file a motion to dismiss, and charges against your client are dropped. You then file a civil rights action against the arresting officer in federal court alleging unlawful arrest. As a defense, the officer's attorney argues that the arrest was not unlawful because the ordinance is susceptible to a more limited constitutional construction than that given by the Massachusetts Supreme Court. How do you respond?

Case 4:

Your client, after standing on a highway overpass with a large sign saying "Osama bin Laden Is Still Alive," was charged with violating a state statute that prohibits "any person from displaying any sign or picture that stops or impedes vehicular or pedestrian traffic." The charges were eventually dropped, but your client has refrained from participating in any more demonstrations due to fear from arrest.

You determine that:

- The statute has not been narrowed by any construction of the state supreme court.

- While other arrests have been made under the statute, no one has been prosecuted for a violation.

Can you successfully assert a vagueness challenge to the statute in federal court?

Can you successfully assert an overbreadth challenge to the statute in federal court?

Chapter 8

PUBLIC EMPLOYEE SPEECH RIGHTS

INTRODUCTION

Public employee speech cases arise in an "enormous variety of fact situations" in which a governmental employer fires or disciplines an employee because of his or her expression. *Pickering v. Board of Education*, 391 U.S. 563, 569 (1968). The Supreme Court's decisions have considered such varied circumstances as writing a letter to the editor of the local paper, providing an internal school memorandum to a local radio station for public broadcast, complaining of racial discrimination privately to a superior at work, preparing and distributing an unauthorized internal office questionnaire regarding employee morale, expressing privately to a co-worker a desire for a successful presidential assassination, accepting honoraria for articles and speaking engagements, and moonlighting by selling sexually explicit videotapes on eBay. The expression at issue can thus take place either at work or after working hours, as long as the employer uses the expression as the basis for employment-related discipline.

Public employee speech cases typically reach a private attorney after the public employee has been terminated or disciplined. The attorney must investigate whether the disciplinary action is due to constitutionally protected employee expression. Attorneys for the government then defend any resulting suit, although occasionally the public employer has the foresight to seek legal advice before terminating or disciplining the employee for expressive activities.

Until the middle of the twentieth century, public employees did not have constitutional protection from restrictions placed on the exercise of their constitutional expressive rights by governmental employers. But in a series of cases beginning in the 1950s, the Court began to limit the government's authority to condition public employment on the employee's political associations. *Pickering v. Board of Education* extended this principle to other forms of expression by public employees, holding a public school teacher could not be fired for criticizing the school board's proposals to raise revenue in a letter to the editor of the local newspaper. *Pickering* determined that public employees should not lose their precious First Amendment rights by virtue of government employment. Nevertheless, the Court recognized that the government's interests as an employer "differ significantly from those it possesses in connection with regulation of the speech of the citizenry in general." 391 U.S. at 568. The judiciary therefore must "arrive at a balance between the interests of the [public employee], as a citizen, in commenting upon matters of public concern and the interest of the State, as an employer, in promoting the efficiency of the public services it performs through its employees." *Id.*

In order to effectuate this balance, the expression of public employees is protected from job retaliation under the First Amendment only if a number of hurdles are satisfied. First, only employees who speak "as a citizen" are protected, which means that there is no constitutional protection from employer discipline for statements made pursuant to an employee's "official duties." *Garcetti v. Ceballos*, 547 U.S. 410, 421 (2006). Second, to be protected, the expression must address a "matter of public concern." *Connick v. Myers*, 461 U.S. 138, 147 (1983). Assuming the first two hurdles are satisfied, the third step balances the state's interest in providing efficient governmental services against the individual and public interests in the speech at issue. *Pickering*, 391 U.S. at 568. The fourth and final inquiry then analyzes as a factual matter whether the speech was the basis for the adverse employment action, providing the government an opportunity to avoid liability if it establishes that it would have undertaken the same action irrespective of the employee's protected speech. *Mount Healthy City School District Board of Education v. Doyle*, 429 U.S. 274, 285–87 (1977).

The first inquiry, whether the speech was made pursuant to an employee's job duties, has caused some confusion in the lower courts. The Supreme Court first adopted this requirement in its 2006 *Garcetti* decision, which is the only high court decision to date addressing the issue. Yet *Garcetti* unfortunately did not provide much guidance on ascertaining the scope of an employee's duties, other than rejecting the premise that employers can confidently rely on "excessively broad descriptions." 547 U.S. at 424–25. The Court explained that listing a particular task in a formal job description, which often does not resemble the employee's actual duties, is "neither necessary nor sufficient" to constitute official duty unprotected speech. Instead, the query is a "practical one." *Id.* But several approaches to this "practical" query are possible.

One approach is to interpret *Garcetti* narrowly to apply only to speech that "the employer itself has commissioned or created." *Id.* at 421-22. Under this view, only expression that is required by the job, or that is part of the expected tasks of the employee, is outside the ambit of the First Amendment. *Cf. Posey v. Lake Pend Oreille School District No. 84*, 546 F.3d 1121, 1127 n.2 (9th Cir. 2008). Expression the employee undertakes on his or her own initiative, even if the expression concerns occupational issues or derives from knowledge or experience acquired from professional duties, is subject to protection as citizen speech.

But a diametrically opposed approach considers any employee speech related to the tasks performed on the job unprotected. If the employee's expression derives from special knowledge or experience acquired on the job, this interpretation of *Garcetti* bars any constitutional protection. *Cf. Gorum v. Sessoms*, 561 F.3d 179, 185-86 (3d Cir. 2009). Yet such a broad approach is in tension with some of the precedents reaffirmed in *Garcetti*, such as *Givhan v. West Line Consolidated School District*, 439 U.S. 410, 414 (1979), which held that a public school teacher's complaints to her principal, based on the school's racial discrimination in hiring teachers, were protected from retaliation.

An alternative approach entails an examination of several contextual factors to ascertain whether the expression is made as a citizen, such as the employee's written job description, the locale of the speech, the audience for the speech, the subject matter of the speech, and the ability of citizens who are not governmental employees to engage in analogous expression. *See, e.g., Rohrbough v. University of Colorado Hospital Authority*, 596 F.3d 741, 746-47 (10th Cir. 2010); *Weintraub v. Board of Education*, 593 F.3d 196, 202-05 (2d Cir. 2010); *Abdur-Rahman v. Walker*, 567 F.3d 1278, 1282-86 (11th Cir. 2009); *Davis v. McKinney*, 518 F.3d 304, 313-17 (5th Cir. 2008); *Weisbarth v. Geauga Park District*, 499 F.3d 538, 544-46 (6th Cir. 2007). Such factors seek to ensure that government employees are not silenced in their ability to participate in public affairs, while granting the employer the ability to manage and supervise expression owing its existence to the employer. *See Garcetti*, 547 U.S. at 421-24. Although a majority of the circuits examine such contextual factors, the weight given to the various factors, and the results in each case, vary. Because the Supreme Court has not resolved the appropriate approach, litigants must determine whether binding precedent exists in their jurisdiction and, if not, be prepared to develop their case under alternative approaches.

The second inquiry in public employee speech retaliation claims, whether the speech addresses a matter of public concern, is not as indeterminate. A matter of public concern includes any "matter of political, social, or other concern to the community." *Connick*, 461 U.S. at 146-47. This determination is made from "the content, form, and context of a given statement, as revealed by the whole record." *Id.* at 147-48. Examples of matters of public concern include governmental wrongdoing or breach of public trust, constitutional violations, the appropriate allocation of resources, the government's need for additional revenue, and discrimination in hiring. *See id.* at 146-49 (detailing examples from prior cases). On the other hand, a mere employee grievance or dispute regarding internal office policies does not rise to the level of public concern that must be weighed against governmental interests. *Id.*

The third inquiry then balances the state's interest in providing efficient governmental services against the individual and public interests in the speech at issue. *Pickering*, 391 U.S. at 568. In making this determination, courts must be cognizant of the employer's need to maintain discipline over its employees and to promote harmony among coworkers. *Id.* at 570. Especially when close working relationships are necessary to fulfill governmental responsibilities, the judiciary often defers to the employer's need to manage the office. *Connick*, 461 U.S. at 151-52. But expressive restrictions on public employees must be "necessary" for the government to provide efficient and effective services to the public. *Garcetti*, 547 U.S. at 419. A public employee is still a citizen, retaining a strong individual interest in engaging in expressive activities. Moreover, there is a vital public interest in the "free and unhindered debate on matters of public importance," the core value underlying the Free Speech Clause. *Pickering*, 391 U.S. at 573. Public employees, as a result of their positions, often are likely to have "informed and definite" opinions as to governmental operations, which often influence the electorate's public debate. *Id.* at 572. Such individual and societal interests must be weighed against the government's interests in each case under the facts and circumstances presented.

The final inquiry analyzes whether the speech was the basis for the adverse employment action under the burden shifting approach outlined in *Mount Healthy*, 429 U.S. at 285-87. The employee has the initial burden to show that his or her constitutionally protected expression was a "substantial" or "motivating" factor in the adverse employment action taken by the government. *Id.* at 287. Once the employee satisfies that burden, however, the government can avoid liability by proving, under a preponderance of the evidence, that it would have undertaken the same action even in the absence of the employee's protected expression. *Id.* This final inquiry is an issue of fact, while the first three elements are ultimately questions of law (although the resolution of these ultimate legal issues, according to some lower courts, may depend on subsidiary factual matters). In any event, a thorough understanding of both the law governing public employee speech lawsuits and the facts in a given scenario are necessary in pursuing and defending such claims.

EXERCISE 8

You are an attorney in private practice approached by John Smith. Mr. Smith had been employed as a bookkeeper in a local county tax collection department in California. He subsequently reported his belief that a co-worker was swindling the department of a large amount of money. Like all other county employees, he is required by his employee handbook to "disclose waste, fraud, abuse, and corruption to appropriate authorities." But soon after his report, he is terminated by his employer. He comes to you seeking your advice as to whether he has a claim for wrongful termination.

REQUIRED TASKS:

Task 1:   Research the applicable Ninth Circuit precedents governing Mr. Smith's right to recover.

Task 2:   Prepare a list of additional information that you need to develop from Mr. Smith concerning his claim before representing him.

Task 3:   Assuming that you develop enough information to represent Mr. Smith, draft a set of discovery requests to the government for his case (the LexisNexis Web Course contains forms for the discovery requests that have been started for you).

PRACTICE SKILLS UTILIZED:

Skill 1:   Legal research
Skill 2:   Legal analysis
Skill 3:   Strategic thinking
Skill 4:   Legal drafting

ESTIMATED TIME FOR COMPLETION: Approximately 2 hours

LEVEL OF DIFFICULTY (1 TO 5):

Practice Tip: Your discovery requests should in large part mirror the legal elements of the claim identified in your legal research. Some astute attorneys draft an initial proposed jury charge or proposed conclusions of law before engaging in any discovery to ensure that their discovery requests obtain all the necessary information for each element of their client's claims.

Chapter 9

PUBLIC SCHOOL STUDENTS' SPEECH RIGHTS

INTRODUCTION

Public school students do not "shed their constitutional rights to freedom of speech or expression at the schoolhouse gate." *Tinker v. Des Moines Independent School District*, 393 U.S. 503, 506 (1969). Nevertheless, due to the special characteristics and purpose of the school environment, "the constitutional rights of students in public school are not automatically coextensive with the rights of adults in other settings." *Bethel School District No. 403 v. Fraser*, 478 U.S. 675, 682 (1986). As a result, resolving a free speech claim asserted by a public school student requires balancing the expressive rights of the student against the interests of his or her classmates and the government in creating a meaningful and secure educational environment.

Public school speech cases arise when a school adopts or enforces a policy prohibiting specified student expression, or a public school official disciplines or penalizes a student based on the student's expressive activities. Although the cases usually involve expression occurring either at school or during school-sponsored extracurricular activities, some cases have addressed off-campus expression directed at a school teacher or administrator, such as belittling or threatening references to school officials on a website or blog. Whether the offending speech occurs on or off campus, the attorney for the school district typically learns of the controversy through a school administrator, with the parents or guardians of the student obtaining representation for their child.

In a series of four cases, the Supreme Court has established a framework for analyzing restrictions on student speech in public schools. First, in *Tinker*, the Supreme Court held that regulation of public school student speech was appropriate when "conduct by the student, in class or out of it, which for any reason — whether it stems from time, place, or type of behavior — materially disrupts classwork or involves substantial disorder or invasion of the rights of others." *Tinker*, 393 U.S. at 513. There, students were punished for wearing black armbands to school in protest of the Vietnam War. While the armbands had caused discussion and controversy, there was no showing of a disruption of the school day. The Court explained that "a mere desire to avoid the discomfort and unpleasantness that always accompany an unpopular viewpoint" was not enough to ban student speech. *Id.* at 509. Consequently, the school officials' actions violated the students' First Amendment free speech rights.

Second, in *Fraser*, the Court upheld discipline of a high school student who had made sexually suggestive remarks during a student election assembly. While there was no disruption of school operations to satisfy the *Tinker* rule, the Court nonetheless held that school officials were justified in sanctioning sexually explicit student speech made during a school event. *Fraser*, 478 U.S. at 685 ("A high school assembly or classroom is no place for a sexually explicit monologue directed towards an unsuspecting audience of teenage students."). The question after *Fraser* was whether the holding was limited to sex-themed student speech, or whether school officials had wider latitude to discipline speech deemed "offensive."

Third, in *Hazelwood School District v. Kuhlmeier*, 484 U.S. 260, 273 (1988), the Court held that educators could restrict speech sponsored by the school or that could be fairly characterized as part of the school curriculum if the restriction was "reasonably related to legitimate pedagogical concerns." The case involved students working on a school newspaper to earn credit for their high school journalism class. School officials pulled two pages of articles from the newspaper on account of the students' failure to follow journalistic best practices, such as providing the subject of a story the opportunity to respond. *Id.* at 275 & n.8. The Court held that the student newspaper was part of the school curriculum because the students earned academic credit for their work, student work on the newspaper was intended to teach content in the journalism curriculum, and school officials retained final approval over the newspaper's content. *Id.* at 268-70. Also, pulling the articles was "reasonably related" to the school's interest in teaching the students to follow professional journalistic standards.

Fourth, in *Morse v. Frederick*, 551 U.S. 393 (2007), the Court upheld student discipline for speech made during a school-sponsored event that promoted illegal drug use. High school officials had organized an event for students to assemble in front of the school building to watch a runner carrying the Olympic torch. During the event, several students held up a banner with the words "BONG HiTS 4 JESUS." The students conceded that the banner was not a political protest, saying only that they considered the banner's message to be silly nonsense intended to draw attention. The Court found that school officials could have reasonably interpreted the banner as promoting illegal drug use, and that school officials have a strong interest in barring such messages from school events. Indeed, the Court stated that "deterring drug use by schoolchildren is an 'important — indeed, perhaps compelling' interest." *Id.*

Morse also clarified the scope of the Court's holding in *Fraser.* Specifically, the Court in *Morse* explained that school officials may not prohibit or sanction student speech that they merely find offensive. *Id.* (*Fraser* "should not be read to encompass any speech that could fit under some definition of 'offensive.'"). While the Court did not further elaborate on *Fraser*, *id.* ("[t]he mode of analysis employed in *Fraser* is not entirely clear"), it leaves that case most likely limited to sexually suggestive student speech made in the classroom or during a school event.

These cases leave several unanswered questions. When is a school activity part of the school curriculum? What must be shown for a material and substantial disruption of school operations? When does disruptive student behavior unacceptably interfere with the rights of third parties? What other topics, if any, should school officials be permitted to prohibit in the name or protecting student health and safety? Both school administrators and attorneys frequently grapple with such problems.

EXERCISE 9

You are the attorney for the North Valley School District. The District Superintendent is considering whether to initiate disciplinary proceedings against a student at the North Valley High School for a parody dating profile that the student created under the name of the high school principal. When the Superintendent met with the student's parents to discuss the parody dating profile, the parents mentioned that they had contacted a local attorney because they were concerned that the District might be infringing their son's First Amendment rights. As the Superintendent decides whether to refer the student for a disciplinary hearing, she would like your opinion whether discipline would violate the student's First Amendment right to free speech. The Superintendent has sent you the following Memo with that request.

MEMORANDUM

To: District Counsel
From: Mary Hanes, Superintendent
Re: Possible Student Discipline for Parody Dating Profile

As we discussed yesterday, I must decide by next week whether to refer John Douglas, a junior at the High School, for a disciplinary hearing for the parody dating profile he created in the name of the high school principal, David Renfro. You asked that I write a Memo summarizing the situation.

About two weeks ago, Principal Renfro sent me an e-mail message with a link to a dating profile on a private, adult dating website that purported to be for him. The profile was in the name "David Renfro," and under occupation, it stated "Large and In Charge at North Valley High School." The profile picture was Principal Renfro's picture from the High School web page. The profile asks for answers to specific questions, and the following are some of the questions and answers listed in the fake profile:

Question: Do you smoke?

Answer: Oh yeah! I'm high as a kite 24/7!

Question: Do you drink alcohol?

Answer: You betcha! Got a big ol' keg behind my desk!

Question: Have you dated in the past month?

Answer: Had a threesome with the prom king and queen!

Question: What is your birthday?

Answer: Too drunk to remember, dude.

Principal Renfro's e-mail message stated that he learned about the fake profile from an anonymous note that provided the web link, and stated that "the student body is abuzz about this." The note also explained that a junior, John Douglas, was bragging about having created the fake profile.

The day after receiving the anonymous note, Principal Renfro confronted John about the fake profile. John initially denied creating the profile, but then admitted doing so after he was shown the anonymous note. John explained that he had created the fake profile on his home computer, and he then sent text messages with a link to his friends to let them know about it. In addition to bragging about the fake dating profile at school, John also used school computers to show the fake profile to fellow students. Principal Renfro directed John to take down the profile, and told John that he would have to report the incident to the Superintendent for possible discipline.

About one week after receiving Principal Renfro's e-mail message, I sent a letter to John and his parents that asked them to meet with me and Principal Renfro to discuss the fake dating profile. The letter informed them that the District was considering bringing a disciplinary action against John for violating the following provisions of the District's Student Code of Conduct:

Disrespect: Harassment of a school administrator via computer/internet with remarks that have demeaning implications.

Gross misbehavior: Obscene, vulgar and profane language.

Computer Policy violation: Use of school pictures without authorization.

A student found to violate these provisions could receive a variety of sanctions up to and including expulsion. During our meeting, John's parents let me know that they had brought my letter to a local attorney, and that the attorney explained that any discipline of John for using his home computer to post the fake dating profile would likely violate John's First Amendment speech rights.

As we discussed, before deciding whether to refer John for a disciplinary hearing, I would like your opinion about the First Amendment issue raised by the attorney consulted by John's parents. Please let me know if you need any additional information.

REQUIRED TASKS:

Task 1:   Reply to the Superintendent's request for your opinion on the First Amendment free speech issue. Please put your opinion in the form of a memorandum to the Superintendent.

Task 2:   As part of your memorandum, ask for additional helpful information that you would need for a complete legal analysis.

PRACTICE SKILLS UTILIZED:

Skill 1:   Legal analysis and writing
Skill 2:   Strategic thinking

ESTIMATED TIME FOR COMPLETION: Approximately 1-1½ hours

LEVEL OF DIFFICULTY (1 TO 5):

Chapter 10

GOVERNMENT SPEECH

INTRODUCTION

Government speech occurs when the government advances its own message in the First Amendment marketplace of ideas. Governmental officials or agencies frequently engage in expression in an attempt to garner public support for governmental policies. In other situations, the government funds or otherwise supports speech by private actors, but only on the condition that the expression of these private persons advances the government's position. Such viewpoint-based funding and support is authorized when the government is itself the speaker because the government is ultimately "accountable to the electorate and the political process for its advocacy. If the citizenry objects, newly elected officials later could espouse some different or contrary position." *Board of Regents v. Southworth*, 529 U.S. 217, 235 (2000). Government speech is thus not regulated by the judiciary under the free speech guarantee of the First Amendment, but instead is predominantly regulated by the people through the political process.

The distinction between government speech and private speech is therefore critical. Although sometimes this distinction is self-evident, such as when a governmental official expresses a view through governmentally controlled channels, in other instances, such as when the government funds private expression, the distinction is fuzzy. How much weight should be placed on the identity of the literal speaker? How important is governmental or private editorial control over the message at issue? Is the source of funding for the speech dispositive? Should the distinction between government and private speech depend on an objective standard focusing on whether the reasonable observer would attribute the speech to the government, a subjective standard relying on the underlying purposes of the expression, or both objective and subjective standards?

Because government speech as a distinct free speech concept has only recently been acknowledged by the courts, many of these issues have not been definitively resolved. As Justice Souter remarked in *Johanns v. Livestock Marketing Association*, 544 U.S. 550, 574 (2005) (Souter, J., dissenting), the government speech doctrine is "relatively new, and correspondingly imprecise," with only a relatively handful of Supreme Court decisions addressing its scope.

Johanns involved a challenge by beef associations and producers to the Beef Promotion and Research Act, which imposed an assessment on the sale and importation of beef to fund promotional advertisements for the beef industry. The promotional campaigns were designed by an operating committee evenly split between governmental and private appointees. *Id.* at 560. Its advertisements typically bore the attribution "Funded by America's Beef Producers," without specifying the government's involvement. *Id.* at 554-55. Nevertheless, the Supreme Court held that the promotional message was "from beginning to end the message established by the Federal Government." *Id.* at 560. The Court reasoned that the Secretary of Agriculture exercised final approval authority over each word in the campaign, members of the Department of Agriculture participated in formulating the promotional proposals, the government established the overarching message to be communicated, and the government funded the program through an assessment on cattle sales and importation. *Id.* at 561–62. So even though the development and expression of the government's specific message was assisted by nongovernmental actors, and the government's participation was not readily evident to the reasonable observer, the promotional campaigns still entailed the expression of the government based on its establishment and control of the message.

The government can also invoke the government speech doctrine when it uses private speakers to transmit messages related to a government program. Thus, in *Rust v. Sullivan*, 500 U.S. 173, 192-200 (1991), the Supreme Court upheld regulations barring recipients of federal funding for family planning counseling from providing abortion-related advice, reasoning that the government could convey its own message preferring childbirth over abortion through the program it created and funded. Yet mere governmental funding alone is insufficient if the government disclaims responsibility for the resulting expression. For example, in *Rosenberger v. Rectors & Visitors of the University of Virginia*, 515 U.S. 819, 834-35 (1995), the Court held that the funds the university provided to student organizations were not government speech when the university disclaimed responsibility and control over the qualifying student groups and their subsequent expression.

Government speech may also exist when the expression originates with a private source and the government subsequently accepts the expression as its own. In *Pleasant Grove City v. Summum*, 555 U.S. 460, 472 (2009), for instance, the Court held that the government's acceptance and display of privately financed and donated monuments constituted government speech. The Court reasoned that viewers typically and reasonably interpreted such monuments as expressing a message on the property owner's behalf, since property owners did not typically permit the display of permanent monuments advancing messages contrary to their beliefs. The Court buttressed this reasoning by highlighting the typical governmental practice of "selective receptivity" of privately donated monuments, under which governments historically have refused to accept and display those monuments that contravene factors such as esthetics, traditions, and culture. *Id.* In accepting a monument, then, the government is expressing its own message, which is not subject to scrutiny under the Free Speech Clause.

Yet these few Supreme Court pronouncements have not provided much guidance to the lower courts in distinguishing private speech from government speech. Some courts primarily emphasize editorial control, while other courts employ a variety of factors when evaluating whether speech is private or state-sponsored. Until the Supreme Court provides more guidance in the area, litigants and courts confront a challenge in deciding whether certain expression constitutes government speech. All that is certain is, if the expression is government speech, the government may exercise complete control over the message, without providing any support for opposing viewpoints.

EXERCISE 10

Specialty license plates, which are available for purchase and contain a specialized design and slogan, are issued by almost every state. Many states have authorized more than a hundred different specialty plates, including ones for colleges and universities, military and veterans groups, civic and professional organizations, professional sports teams, public servants, and issue advocacy groups. Some examples include:

The state typically charges an extra $25–$50 per year for the plates, with the proceeds frequently split between the state treasury and some type of fund benefitting the private organization. Many states create the plates based on designs submitted by defined eligible institutions, which usually pay an application fee and provide either prepaid orders or evidence that a specified number of individuals will likely purchase the plates.

But this relatively open process in many states has led to litigation when requests for specialty plates are denied. As one example, some states have resisted a requested design by the Sons of Confederate Veterans that includes a Confederate flag. Other states have refused to issue a pro-choice specialty plate, even while offering a pro-life specialty plate. And certain organizations, such as the Ku Klux Klan, are usually entirely excluded from the process.

The courts have reached conflicting decisions regarding whether such specialty license plates are private speech or government speech. *Compare, e.g., Arizona Life Coalition, Inc. v. Stanton*, 515 F.3d 956, 965–68 (9th Cir. 2008) (private speech) & *Sons of Confederate Veterans, Inc. v. Commissioner of the Virginia Department of Motor Vehicles*, 288 F.3d 610, 621 (4th Cir. 2002) (private speech), *with ACLU of Tennessee v. Bredesen*, 441 F.3d 370, 375 (6th Cir. 2006) (government speech). If the specialty license plates are government speech, the state has no obligation to authorize plates with viewpoints with which it does not agree. But if the specialty plates are private speech, viewpoint discrimination would be forbidden, unless perhaps strict scrutiny could be satisfied.

You are a legislator in a state that does not currently have a specialty license plate program, but would like to develop such a program as a method to increase state revenues. The state wants to ensure that its license plates are government speech so that it can control the messages disseminated and will be less likely to have a lawsuit filed against it. A proposed bill regarding the specialty license plate program provides as follows:

A Bill To Be Entitled An Act
Relating to a Specialty License Program

Be it enacted by the Legislature:

(1) The State Department of Motor Vehicles shall issue specialty license plates on the application of any organization or group within the state that pays an $8,000 application fee and provides at least 1,000 prepaid $40 orders for the plates.

(2) The organization or group that is seeking the specialty license plate shall submit a design for the plate to the State Department of Motor Vehicles.

(3) The Director of the State Department of Motor Vehicles may refuse to issue a specialty license plate that the Director considers objectionable to one or more members of the public.

(4) Additional specialty license plates will be issued to members of the organization or group upon individual application and payment of the $40 fee.

(5) The Director may adopt rules to implement and administer this Act.

How would you revise this proposed legislation to make it as likely as possible that the specialty license program will be viewed as government speech?

REQUIRED TASKS:

Task 1:   Identify the factors that will make a judicial determination that the specialty plate program is government speech more likely.

Task 2:   Revise the proposed bill regarding the program to make it more likely to be viewed as government speech.

PRACTICE SKILLS UTILIZED:

Skill 1:   Legal analysis
Skill 2:   Statutory drafting and editing

ESTIMATED TIME FOR COMPLETION: Approximately 45 minutes

LEVEL OF DIFFICULTY (1 TO 5):

Practice Tip: The LexisNexis Web Course contains links to relevant cases and offers multiple choice questions for review.

Chapter 11

FREEDOM OF EXPRESSIVE ASSOCIATION

INTRODUCTION

While the text of the First Amendment does not explicitly protect a right of expressive association, the freedom to associate for the purpose of advancing ideas and airing grievances is a necessary adjunct to freedom of speech, the right to peaceably assemble, and the right to petition for redress of grievances. *NAACP v. Alabama ex rel. Patterson*, 357 U.S. 449, 460 (1958). Without the ability to gather with like-minded individuals to engage in First Amendment activity, the protected expressive rights would lose much of their practical significance. Thus, implicit within the other rights protected by the First Amendment is "a corresponding right to associate with others in pursuit of a wide variety of political, social, economic, educational, religious, and cultural ends." *Roberts v. United States Jaycees*, 468 U.S. 609, 622 (1984).

Because the freedom of expressive association is a correlative right, it arises in a variety of contexts. In some cases, the government attempts to compel a private association, such as the NAACP, to reveal the identity of its members, which the Supreme Court held is impermissible unless necessary to serve some compelling governmental interest. *NAACP*, 357 U.S. at 460–61. The government has also threatened public employees with termination unless they divulged the organizations to which they belonged, but this is likewise improper unless membership in the organization relates to employees' fitness and competency for their position. *Shelton v. Tucker*, 364 U.S. 479, 485–88 (1960). The government on other occasions seeks to regulate the internal conduct of private associations, including precluding the association from undertaking specified activities, penalizing the association in some manner for its conduct, or banning discrimination in the association's membership on the basis of sexual orientation, gender, race, religion or similar criteria. The association may then challenge such regulations as violating its right of expressive association, requiring the government to establish that any significant interference with the association's expression is necessary to serve a compelling governmental interest unrelated to the suppression of speech. *Boy Scouts of America v. Dale*, 530 U.S. 640, 648 (2000). The freedom of expressive association also provides protection for political parties, preventing the government from substantially burdening their associational rights unless strict scrutiny is satisfied. *California Democratic Party v. Jones*, 530 U.S. 567, 574–82 (2000).

Despite the number of ways in which the issue arises, strict scrutiny is only appropriate if (1) the organization is an expressive association, and (2) the government has significantly interfered with its expression in some manner. Otherwise, a rational basis or reasonableness standard will be applied, which does not provide much protection.

For heightened scrutiny to apply, a group first must establish that it is an expressive association. While expressive associations are not limited to advocacy groups, the organization must engage in some form of expression protected by the First Amendment as a means to further political, social, economic, educational, religious, cultural, or other similar ends. *Dale*, 530 U.S. at 648; *Roberts*, 468 U.S. at 622. A collective public or private expressive effort supporting some shared goal is necessary, even though the overarching purpose of the association does not have to be to disseminate a particular message. *Dale*, 530 U.S. at 648, 655; *Roberts*, 468 U.S. at 622. The Supreme Court has recognized a wide variety of groups as expressive associations, including political parties, the Boy Scouts, the NAACP, the Jaycees, and other similar organizations. *See, e.g.*, *Dale*, 530 U.S. at 648-50; *Jones*, 530 U.S. at 574; *Roberts*, 468 U.S. at 622; *NAACP*, 357 U.S. at 458-63.

The expressive association next must demonstrate a governmental intrusion that significantly interferes with its message. Such a significant governmental intrusion can take the form of imposing penalties on the group or its members due to the group's expression, requiring the group to disclose previously anonymous members, or interfering with the internal affairs of the organization, such as its membership requirements or its choice of officers or nominees. *See Roberts*, 468 U.S. at 622-23. But not all governmental interferences with an expressive association are considered significant. For instance, the government may prohibit certain expressive associations from adopting discriminatory membership policies if the acceptance of members on a nondiscriminatory basis does not impair their ability to express their views. *See New York State Club Association, Inc. v. City of New York*, 487 U.S. 1, 13 (1988). Moreover, the government may condition governmental forum benefits to expressive associations on viewpoint neutral criteria. *Christian Legal Society v. Martinez*, 130 S. Ct. 2971, 2985-86 (2010). And governmental regulations regarding the electoral process for political parties are typically permissible, as long as the regulations do not significantly intrude on political parties' ability to select their chosen candidates. *See Jones*, 530 U.S. at 572-82. Yet if the governmental regulation constitutes a significant interference with the expressive association's message, the government must prove the intrusion is necessary to serve a compelling interest unrelated to suppressing the group's expression.

This requires both that the governmental interest is compelling and the regulation is no more extensive than necessary to accomplish the government's objective without significantly impairing the expressive association's views. *Roberts*, 468 U.S. at 623-28. The Court has recognized that the government may have a compelling interest unrelated to the suppression of expression in eradicating gender and other forms of discrimination, which justifies a governmentally mandated nondiscrimination policy that does not unduly interfere with the association's expression. *See id.* But this interest does not extend to severely hampering the association's ability to express itself. *Dale*, 530 U.S. at 659. The group's expression and the extent of the governmental intrusion on its expression are thus the key factors in evaluating an expressive association claim.

EXERCISE 11

Your client, Bif Boyd, has been criminally charged with hazing. The indictment reads as follows:

IN THE 99th CRIMINAL JUDICIAL COURT
STATE OF MARSCH

STATE OF MARSCH v. BIF BOYD	Violations of Penal Code § 33.03

INDICTMENT

The Grand Jury charges:

Background:

1. The defendant, BIF BOYD ("Boyd"), is the fraternity pledge master of the Alpha Alpha Alpha male service fraternity at Mason College, a private university in Marsch. In this position, he arranges all events involving the provisional new members of the fraternity, referred to as "pledges."

2. Boyd heavily advertised an event on October 10 for the pledges of Alpha Alpha Alpha to clean the bear pits maintained by Mason College, posting fliers all around the campus encouraging students to watch the pledges perform "menial labor" by "cleaning the dung" of the campus mascots.

3. A significant crowd gathered on October 10 to watch the cleaning of the bear pits by the pledges. A number of members in the audience began heckling and tormenting the pledges mercilessly as they worked.

4. Several pledges asked Boyd if they could quit, but Boyd said that if they did so, they would not become full members of Alpha Alpha Alpha.

5. Bif then required the pledges to shout, "By serving others, we do the best for ourselves," while they worked.

6. One pledge, Heath Wimple, collapsed soon after being required to shout while working as he was being heckled by the members of the audience. He was taken to receive medical attention and diagnosed as having suffered from a combination of dehydration and elevated stress levels.

Count 1

7. The above-described actions constitute hazing under Marsch Penal Code § 33.03(A)(2).

8. Boyd committed an intentional, knowing, or reckless act, on the campus of Mason College, that endangered the mental or physical health of Heath Wimple, by requiring him to continue to work at the bear pits and to shout during the bear pit clean-up if he wanted to become a full member of Alpha Alpha Alpha.

9. This physical activity subjected Heath Wimple to an unreasonable risk of harm and adversely affected his mental or physical health.

10. Boyd thereby engaged in hazing as prohibited by MPC § 33.03(A)(2).

Count 2

11. The above-described actions constitute hazing under Marsch Penal Code § 33.03(A)(4).

12. Boyd's intentional, knowing, or reckless act of requiring Heath Wimple to continue to work at the bear pits and to shout during the bear pit clean-up subjected Heath Wimple to extreme mental stress, shame, or humiliation, and adversely affected his mental health or dignity.

13. Boyd thereby engaged hazing as prohibited by MPC § 33.03(A)(4).

DATED: October 19   A TRUE BILL

Judson Bend   David Donovan
District Attorney   Foreperson

Marsch Penal Code § 33.03 — Hazing

(A) Hazing is any intentional, knowing, or reckless act, occurring on or off the campus of an educational institution, by one person alone or acting with others, directed against a student, that endangers the mental or physical health or safety of a student for the purpose of pledging, being initiated into, affiliating with, holding office in, or maintaining membership in any organization whose members are or include students at an educational institution. Hazing includes

   (1) any type of physical brutality, such as whipping, beating, striking, branding, shocking, or similar activity;

   (2) any type of physical activity, such as sleep deprivation, exposure to the elements, calisthenics, or other activity that subjects the student to an unreasonable risk of harm or that adversely affects the mental or physical health of the student;

   (3) any activity involving consumption of food, liquid, alcoholic beverage, liquor, drug, or other substance which subjects the student to an unreasonable risk of harm or which adversely affects the mental or physical health of the student; or

   (4) any activity that intimidates or threatens the student with ostracism, that subjects the student to extreme mental stress, shame, or humiliation, or that adversely affects the mental health or dignity of the student.

(B) A person commits an offense if the person:

   (1) engages in hazing;

   (2) solicits, encourages, directs, aids, or attempts to aid another in engaging in hazing;

(3)   recklessly permits hazing to occur; or

(4)   has firsthand knowledge of a specific hazing incident and fails to report that knowledge in writing to the dean of students or other appropriate official of the institution.

(C)   Any person who commits the offense of hazing shall be guilty of a third-degree felony.

ADDITIONAL FACTS:

These are the additional facts provided to you by Bif. The philosophy of Alpha Alpha Alpha is that service to others is the mission of humans on Earth. Although there is no particular religious belief required by Alpha Alpha Alpha, all members must commit to its motto: "By serving others, we do the best for ourselves." New members of Alpha Alpha Alpha are selected through an extensive application and interview process to ensure a deeply ingrained desire for service. Once selected, the provisional new member becomes a "pledge" for six weeks and, during this time, must show his commitment to the service of others.

The last event of the six-week pledging period is the semi-annual cleaning of the campus bear pits, which is the home of Mason College's prior bear cub mascots once they become too large to be considered cubs. Before the cleaning, the bears are placed into their cages by their professional handlers. Then, the pledges of Alpha Alpha Alpha are brought into the bear pit to clean up the accumulated waste of the bears and any trash that has been deposited into the pit. The cleaning of the bear pits is a big campus event at Mason College, with students coming out to cheer (and sometimes jeer) the pledges as they commit their last act of service before becoming full-fledged members of Alpha Alpha Alpha.

Bif posted the following flier everywhere around campus before the semi-annual bear cleaning event in order to disseminate the fraternity's message of service:

COME TO THE SEMI-ANNUAL BEAR PIT CLEANING

Sponsored by Alpha Alpha Alpha

"By serving others, we do the best for ourselves"

The Alpha Alpha Alpa pledges will perform the ultimate act of service — cleaning the dung of our mascots so that the bear pits can be enjoyed by all, alumni and students alike.

So come out and give our pledges some support as they perform this menial labor and show that through service we gain our best earthly rewards.

The crowd for the bear pit cleaning was, as Bif hoped, enormous. But the size of the crowd brought out many more hecklers than in years past, and a large, boisterous group of mostly business students barraged the pledges with a constant stream of demeaning torments while they were working. Some of the pledges wanted to quit because of the heckling, but Bif was energized, seeing this as an opportunity to illustrate the benefits of the Alpha Alpha Alpha philosophy, and he told the pledges to shout out as they worked the Alpha Alpha Alpha motto, "By serving others, we do the best for ourselves."

Unfortunately, though, one of the pledges, Heath Wimple, had a nervous breakdown as a result of the heckling and went to receive medical attention. Medical personnel reported the incident to Mason College and the district attorney's office. The district attorney, who was not fond of Mason College, brought the above-indictment against Bif for hazing based on the above-described activities.

REQUIRED TASKS:

Task 1: Draft a motion to dismiss the indictment on constitutional grounds (the LexisNexis Web Course contains a form for the motion that has been started for you).

Task 2: Prepare a list of any other information which would be relevant to the dismissal that needs to be developed.

PRACTICE SKILLS UTILIZED:

Skill 1: Legal analysis
Skill 2: Motion drafting
Skill 3: Strategic thinking

ESTIMATED TIME FOR COMPLETION: Approximately 1½ hours

LEVEL OF DIFFICULTY (1 TO 5):

Chapter 12

THE POLITICAL PROCESS AND THE FIRST AMENDMENT

INTRODUCTION

Political expression is at the core of the First Amendment. Yet the government has compelling reasons to regulate such expression in certain circumstances where it is necessary, for instance, to prevent actual corruption or the appearance of corruption in the political process. The difficulty is determining when laws governing political expression are indeed essential to supporting compelling governmental interests, rather than serving illegitimate concerns such as stifling dissident political expression or protecting incumbents from political rivals. The courts frequently must resolve these issues in cases brought by political parties, campaigns, and activists challenging laws that govern campaign finance and political speech.

The foundational campaign finance case is *Buckley v. Valeo*, 424 U.S. 1, 19–23 (1976), which distinguished contributions to a political candidate from political expenditures. While recognizing that caps on contributions somewhat restrict both political communication and the contributor's ability to support a preferred candidate, the Court reasoned that a reasonable contribution limit only marginally impacts the contributor's symbolic expression of support for the candidate. This marginal impact, the Court continued, must be evaluated in light of the countervailing governmental interests in reducing the probability of corruption and the appearance of corruption frequently inherent in inordinately generous campaign contributions. *Id.* at 26–29. When contribution limits are "closely drawn" to advance such "sufficiently important" interests, the limitations are constitutionally valid. *Id.* A limitation is not closely drawn, however, if it severely impacts political dialogue by preventing the accumulation of the necessary resources for effective advocacy. *Id.* at 21. Yet the Court typically reviews contribution limits deferentially — since *Buckley*, the Court has only invalidated contribution caps in one case, holding Vermont's limits for statewide offices were too low to be closely drawn to the important governmental interests in reducing corruption and the appearance of corruption. *See Randall v. Sorrell*, 548 U.S. 230 (2006).

In contrast, expenditures by a campaign or by independent groups have a closer relationship to political expression without the same connection to corruption, necessitating a more exacting judicial scrutiny of expenditure regulations. *Buckley*, 424 U.S. at 44–58. In comparing contribution and expenditure limitations, *Buckley* reasoned that expenditure caps "impose significantly more severe restrictions on protected freedoms of political expression and association." *Id.* at 23. This is because the restriction on spending reduces the quantity of expression, detrimentally impacting the issues discussed, the depth of their exploration, and the audience reached. *Id.* at 19. At the same time, independent expenditures do not pose the same dangers of real or apparent corruption as hefty campaign contributions. *Id.* at 44-48. *Buckley* therefore held that a sufficient governmental interest did not support capping such expenditures. *Id.* at 44-59. Caps, bans, or other regulations that significantly interfere with independent political expenditures only can be upheld under strict judicial scrutiny, requiring the government to establish that the regulation is necessary to serve a compelling governmental interest. *See Citizens United v. Federal Election Commission*, 558 U.S. 310, 130 S. Ct. 876, 898 (2010).

The same underlying principle applies to other aspects of governmental regulation of the political process, requiring heightened strict scrutiny of laws substantially infringing on the expressive or associational rights of voters or political parties. Sometimes strict scrutiny is satisfied, such as in *Burson v. Freeman*, 504 U.S. 191, 199–202 (1992) (Blackmun, J., plurality op.), which reasoned that compelling governmental interests in preventing voter intimidation and election fraud justified a ban on soliciting votes or displaying or distributing campaign literature within 100 feet of the entrance to a polling place. But in other instances, the Court has reasoned that strict scrutiny is not satisfied. In *Brown v. Hartlage*, 456 U.S. 45, 58–62 (1982), for instance, the Court held that the state could not prohibit a county commissioner candidate from promising during his campaign to serve at a reduced salary. *First National Bank of Boston v. Bellotti*, 435 U.S. 765, 778–95 (1978), held that banks and business corporations could not be precluded from spending money to express their views on ballot initiatives and referenda. And *Citizens United* held that, while the government could regulate the political speech of corporations and unions through disclaimer and disclosure requirements, it could not ban those organizations from using their general funds to make independent political expenditures advocating the election or defeat of a candidate. 130 S. Ct. at 886.

Strict scrutiny also applies to the canons of judicial conduct that regulate the speech of judicial candidates in the approximately forty states that choose at least some of their judges through popular elections. The Supreme Court employed this heightened scrutiny in *Republican Party of Minnesota v. White*, 536 U.S. 765, 775–84 (2002), to invalidate the Minnesota Judicial Code of Conduct's prohibition on a judicial candidate announcing a view on a disputed legal or political issue that might come before the judge. The Supreme Court reasoned that this "announce clause," despite its enactment by a majority of the states, was not narrowly tailored to serve the government's asserted interest in impartiality. A judicial candidate's announcement of a view on an issue, the Court explained, does not impact the judge's ability to fairly dispense justice to the parties, nor would it be any more destructive of judicial open-mindedness than other acceptable avenues of expressing the same thought, such as books or written opinions.

The Court's holding in *White* led many states to hurriedly amend their own judicial conduct codes (links to some of these amended codes are provided on the LexisNexis Web Course). But the question of whether the amended codes satisfy the First Amendment has not been definitively resolved.

EXERCISE 12

After the Supreme Court's decision in *Republican Party of Minnesota v. White*, 536 U.S. 765 (2002), the State of Mayfield revised the Mayfield Code of Judicial Conduct. As revised, the applicable portion of the Code provides:

> A judge or judicial candidate shall not:
>
> (1) make pledges or promises of conduct in office regarding pending or impending cases, specific classes of cases, specific classes of litigants, or specific propositions of law that would suggest to a reasonable person that the judge is predisposed to a probable decision in cases within the scope of the pledge.
>
> (2) make public comment about a pending or impending proceeding which may come before the court in which the judge serves or seeks to serve in a manner which suggests to a reasonable person the judge's probable decision on any particular case.
>
> (3) authorize the public use of his or her name endorsing another candidate for any public office. A judge or judicial candidate may, however, indicate support for a political party, attend political events, and express his or her views on political matters.

A law school classmate and good friend, Charlie Waterman, is running for an elected judicial position in Mayfield. Charlie has just received a questionnaire from a local civic group whose endorsements are often enough to ensure a candidate's victory. Charlie accordingly wants to provide as much information as possible in responding to the questionnaire, but is concerned that certain questions call for responses that may run afoul of the Mayfield Code of Judicial Conduct. Charlie has asked for your help in analyzing some of the questions under the Mayfield Code and, for any questions that may be prohibited, determining whether a First Amendment challenge to the application of the code provision may be warranted. The questions are as follows:

1. In interpreting the Mayfield Constitution, would you promise to strictly construct its text and original meaning, or would you interpret it as a living document that evolves over time?

2. Who are your judicial role models and why do you seek to emulate them?

3. Do you believe the right to trial by jury protected by the Mayfield Constitution has been eroded by the judiciary's increased willingness to enforce arbitration clauses in consumer contracts, employment agreements, and other contracts of adhesion?

4. Who will you support for President of the United States in the next election?

5. Would you promise to uphold all abortion laws unless binding precedent from the Supreme Court of the United States required the law's invalidation?

REQUIRED TASKS:

Task 1:   After studying *White* again, prepare in outline form your opinions
            and supporting rationales regarding whether each question
            violates the Mayfield Code of Judicial Conduct and the likelihood
            of success for a First Amendment challenge to the Code
            provisions.

Task 2:   Research whether answering some of the questions may require
            Charlie Waterman to be recused from certain cases involving
            those issues.

PRACTICE SKILLS UTILIZED:

Skill 1:   Judicial ethical rule analysis
Skill 2:   Case analysis and legal reasoning
Skill 3:   Legal research

ESTIMATED TIME FOR COMPLETION: Approximately 2 hours

LEVEL OF DIFFICULTY (1 TO 5):

Chapter 13

THE NEWSGATHERING FUNCTION AND FREEDOM OF THE PRESS

INTRODUCTION

Aside from defending against liability for libel and other torts, the press has relied on the First Amendment to seek constitutional protection for four other aspects of its work. First, the press has invoked the First Amendment in an attempt to protect its members from disclosing the identity of confidential sources or the information obtained from them. Second, the press has wielded the First Amendment as a sword to seek access to people, places, and proceedings otherwise off-limits to the public. Third, when information has been lawfully obtained, the press has fought legal restrictions on later dissemination of that information. Fourth, the press has argued that the First Amendment bars common law claims related to newsgathering and publishing.

The Supreme Court has recognized that "without some protection for seeking the news, freedom of the press could be eviscerated." Yet newsgathering itself is not afforded absolute constitutional protection. Under *Branzburg v. Hayes*, 408 U.S. 665 (1972), for example, a journalist who refuses to testify about a confidential informant in response to a grand jury subpoena can be held in contempt of court, unless the subpoena is issued to harass the reporter or seeks information beyond what is relevant or material to a grand jury investigation. Nor can the press claim absolute immunity when served with a validly executed search warrant or a request for pretrial discovery in a civil case. According to the Court, the need for disclosure in these circumstances is said to outweigh any resulting burden on newsgathering.

The Court has also declined to afford the press a First Amendment "special right of access" beyond what is available to the public generally. Under this rule, reporters have been denied permission to inspect private areas of a prison facility, conduct face to face interviews with selected prisoners, or copy tape recordings used as evidence in a criminal trial. *See e.g., Pell v. Procunier*, 417 U.S. 817 (1974); *Saxbe v. Washington Post Co.*, 417 U.S. 843 (1974). In limited circumstances, however, a presumptive right of access attaches when "experience and logic" dictate that the proceeding should be open to the public. *Richmond Newspapers, Inc. v. Virginia*, 448 U.S. 555 (1980). Criminal trials, preliminary hearings, and juror voir dire fall into this category, based on an unbroken history of public access and the need to foster public trust in the criminal justice system. These proceedings can only be closed on a case by case basis, upon an explicit finding that closure is narrowly tailored to serve a compelling interest. *See Press Enterprise Co. v. Superior Court*, 464 U.S. 501 (1984); *Globe Newspaper v. Superior Court*, 457 U.S. 596 (1982). Lower federal and state courts have also applied the "experience and logic" test to determine whether the public, and by default the press, has a right to access civil trials, administrative hearings, agency records, and disciplinary proceedings.

In addition to access to judicial proceedings, the Court has recognized the right to publish truthful material that was lawfully obtained from those proceedings. In *Cox Broadcasting Corp. v. Cohn*, 420 U.S. 469, 496 (1975), the Court held that a media company could not be sued for invasion of privacy for publishing the name of a deceased rape victim that a reporter obtained from court documents open to the public. Similarly, in *Florida Star v. BJF*, 491 U.S. 524, (1989), the Court struck down a Florida statute that made a newspaper civilly liable for publishing the name of a rape victim that the newspaper had learned while reading police reports that had been released to the public. *Id.* at 541 ("We hold only that where a newspaper publishes truthful information which it has lawfully obtained, punishment may lawfully be imposed, if at all, only when narrowly tailored to a state interest of the highest order, and that no such interest is satisfactorily served by imposing liability under [the challenged statute] to appellant under the facts of this case."); *see also Smith v. Daily Mail Publishing Co.*, 443 U.S. 97 (1979) (striking down West Virginia statute that made it a crime to publish the name of a juvenile offender). *Bartnicki v. Vopper*, 532 U.S. 514 (2001), extended this line of reasoning beyond information obtained from government records. There, the Court held that members of the media could not be held civilly liable under a federal wiretapping statute for broadcasting an audio recording that the media had obtained lawfully. The original recording itself had been intercepted in violation of the federal statute, and the broadcasters knew or should have known of the illegal interception. The Court, however, held that the broadcasters could not be sanctioned because they had not participated in the illegal interception, and the subject matter of the recording – negotiations between a school district and the teachers' union – was one of public concern. *Id.* at 534-35.

The Court has not allowed the media to escape liability for a broken promise of confidentiality. In *Cohen v. Cowles Media Co.*, 501 U.S. 663 (1991), reporters promised confidentiality to a source in exchange for documents and other information concerning a political campaign. When the newspapers nonetheless published the source's identity, he was fired by his employer. The source then sued the newspapers under promissory estoppel for breach of the promise of confidentiality. The Court held that the First Amendment did not bar the source's civil claim:

> There can be little doubt that the Minnesota doctrine of promissory estoppel is a law of general applicability. It does not target or single out the press. Rather, insofar as we are advised, the doctrine is generally applicable to the daily transactions of all the citizens of Minnesota. The First Amendment does not forbid its application to the press.

Id. at 670.

Practice Tip: Though the Supreme Court has declined to recognize an absolute privilege rooted in the First Amendment, a qualified privilege exists in some jurisdictions. A majority of states have enacted shield statutes to regulate the circumstances under which a reporter can be compelled to testify or to limit the types of evidence that can be seized from the press in response to a warrant. Other states have adopted some form of reporter's privilege under the common law. Some lower courts even interpret *Branzburg* as establishing a qualified privilege that applies unless there is a compelling need for disclosing highly relevant information that cannot be obtained elsewhere. Similarly, statutes and administrative regulations may provide a right of access where one is not constitutionally required.

EXERCISE 13

You represent Alicia Copeland, a reporter with THE NEW VALLEY TIMES, who broke a story on a secret government rendition program. She is seeking advice on a number of issues regarding a government investigation of the program. After reading the article below, how do you advise Copeland in the following situations:

PART 1

Copeland is served with a subpoena to testify and produce documents to the grand jury (copied below). Draft a motion to quash that would protect Copeland from having to appear before the grand jury. In addition to any constitutional arguments, note that under Rule 17(c)(2) of the Federal Rules of Criminal Procedure, a judge may quash or modify a subpoena for documents "if compliance would be unreasonable or oppressive."

PART 2

Following Copeland's interview with Sandra Collins, former Secretary of Defense, regarding the CIA program, she incidentally mentioned her plan to run for President. If Collins is fired from her present job after her supervisor reads about the plan in Copeland's article, can she recover damages in a civil suit against Copeland? What must you ask Copeland in order to answer this question?

PART 3

As a legislative aid in a state that has not enacted a reporter's shield statute, you are asked to draft a bill that strikes an appropriate balance between the needs of a free press and equally important alternative objectives. What does your proposal look like? Referring back to THE NEW VALLEY TIMES article may bring a number of issues into focus. Pay particular attention to the following considerations and be prepared to defend the specifics of your proposal:

- How will your statute define "reporter"?

- What type of information can a reporter keep confidential?

- Are there any requests that a reporter must respond to?

- Does the privilege apply in other circumstances?

- What type of showing, if any, is required to overcome the privilege?

PART 4

In addition to the secret rendition program, Copeland learns that deportation proceedings have been initiated against more than 100 foreign nationals allegedly involved in a human trafficking ring linked to organized crime. Copeland is suspicious of the allegations and decided to attend the deportation hearing to investigate. When she arrives at court, she learns that the Chief Immigration Judge has decided that any deportation proceeding that involves a "heightened security risk" as determined by the Department of Justice will be conducted in secret without access by the press or members of the public. That morning, the Department of Justice had declared that deportation proceedings involving charges of organized crime, like the one Copeland planned to attend, present a "heightened security risk." Copeland wants your advice on whether she has a First Amendment right to attend the proceedings.

Research applicable case law to determine whether Copeland can challenge the closure decision. Your results should yield at least two relevant Supreme Court cases and two lower court cases. How do you use these cases to support or distinguish Copeland's claim? What additional facts will help you better assess the claim?

REQUIRED TASKS:

Task 1:   Draft a Motion to Quash the Grand Jury Subpoena (the LexisNexis Web Course contains a form for the motion that has been started for you).

Task 2:   Investigate additional facts to determine whether Copeland can be held liable for disclosing Collins' plans to run for President.

Task 3:   Draft a proposed reporter's privilege statute that balances the interest in disclosure against the need to protect confidential information.

Task 4:   Research case law to determine whether Copeland has a right to access a closed deportation proceeding.

PRACTICE SKILLS UTILIZED:

Skill 1:   Legal analysis
Skill 2:   Motion drafting
Skill 3:   Factual investigation
Skill 4:   Computer research

ESTIMATED TIME FOR COMPLETION: Approximately 2½ hours

LEVEL OF DIFFICULTY (1 TO 5):

THE NEW VALLEY TIMES

The news you need, when you need it. Since 1947.

Classified Documents Confirm Prisoner Renditions

DOJ Begins Investigation

by Alicia Copeland

A classified government report obtained by the New Valley Times confirms that over 100 individuals detained by the CIA in the war on terrorism were tortured by foreign intelligence agents after being transferred to prisons overseas. The report provides further proof of a secret rendition program that first came to light in 2005.

The prisoners were suspected of having ties to al Qaeda, but the CIA did not have enough evidence to charge them with a crime, an agent familiar with the program said. The President ordered them transferred to countries known to condone torture after routine CIA interrogations failed to produce any tangible leads. The rendition program was set to expire last year but another agent, who spoke on condition of anonymity, said the CIA is still sending prisoners to "torture-camps."

Several military and government oversight blogs are making the same claim. One blog, operated by former Defense Secretary Sandra Collins, says the President used private pilots to transfer prisoners hoping to limit the involvement of military personnel she knew would oppose the program. Collins, who previously defended the use of "any means available" to extract information from potential terrorists, now says she disagrees with the Administration's tactics. It's likely that Collins will take additional steps to distance herself from the current Administration given her plans to run for President in the upcoming election.

The Department of Justice is investigating the existence of the rendition program and whether the treatment of detainees in federal custody violated international law. It also hopes to determine whether government officials unlawfully disclosed classified information about top secret programs.

United States District Court District of Acadia

TO: Alicia Copeland   Subpoena To Testify
                                   Before Grand Jury

                                   Subpoena for:
                                   Person ☒   Documents or
                                                     Objects ☒

YOU ARE HEREBY COMMANDED to appear before the Grand Jury of the United States District Court at the place, date, and time specified below.

| PLACE U.S. District Court 1 Federal Plaza Leland, Acadia 32993 | COURTROOM, DATE AND TIME Grand Jury Room 497 4/24 10:00 a.m. |

YOU ARE ALSO COMMANDED to provide testimony as requested on the following:

1. How you came to possess the classified government report described in the New Valley Times article *Classified Documents Confirm Prisoner Rendition.*

2. The identity of persons interviewed for the article, including but not limited to the person who reported to you that the "CIA did not have enough evidence to charge [the detainees] with a crime," and that "the CIA is still sending prisoners to 'torture camps'."

3. Any and all information related to the existence of a secret rendition program operated by the CIA.

YOU ARE ALSO COMMANDED to bring with you the following documents:

4. Any and all documents you relied on in the course of researching, drafting and revising the above referenced article.

5. Any and all documents relating to conversations you had with Sandra Collins, former Defense Secretary of the United States.

This subpoena shall remain in effect until you are granted leave to depart by the court or by an officer acting on behalf of the court.

| MAGISTRATE JUDGE OR CLERK OF COURT Janice L. Rodriguez, Clerk of Courts By Deputy Clerk S.F. Kurtz | DATE: 3/19 |

This subpoena is issued on application of the

| United States of America K. Bradelman United States Attorney | Attorney Name and Contact K. Bradelman Department of Justice 15 Victory Street Leland, Acadia 32993 |

Chapter 14

THE ESTABLISHMENT CLAUSE

INTRODUCTION

Lawyers who practice in a variety of areas are likely to encounter an Establishment Clause problem at some point. Lawyers who work for public interest organizations represent clients on both sides of the church-state controversy. Organizations like the American Civil Liberties Union, Americans United For Separation of Church and State, and The American Center for Law and Justice have played a major role in shaping Establishment Clause jurisprudence at the Supreme Court through direct client representation or amicus briefs submitted in noteworthy cases. The relationship between lawmakers and public interest lawyers is not always adversarial, however. Government officials often seek the advice of public interest attorneys to ensure that proposed or existing policies and procedures meet constitutional standards.

Establishment Clause cases have also been litigated by lawyers at every level of government. Attorneys with the Department of Justice, for instance, are not only responsible for prosecuting violations of the nation's laws, but also for defending the constitutionality of federal laws challenged in court. The Religious Land Use and Institutionalized Persons Act, Individuals with Disabilities in Education Act, and Elementary and Secondary Education Act are just three of the many federal statutes that have been challenged on Establishment Clause grounds. *See Cutter v. Wilkinson*, 544 U.S. 709 (2005); *Mitchell v. Helms*, 530 U.S. 793 (2000); *Zobrest v. Catalina Foothills School Dist.*, 509 U.S. 1 (1993). Establishment Clause challenges to state or local government action are also common, including challenges to public religious displays, school prayers, or curriculum requirements that mandate the teaching of creationism or "intelligent design" in public school. *See, e.g., Wallace v. Jaffree*, 472 U.S. 38 (1985); *Abington v. Schempp*, 374 U.S. 203 (1963); *Engel v. Vitale*, 370 U.S. 421 (1962); *Croft v. Texas*, 562 F.3d 735 (5th Cir. 2009); *Kitzmiller v. Dover Area School Dist.*, 400 F. Supp. 2d 707 (M.D. Pa. 2005). Attorneys in private practice often handle these cases alongside government lawyers.

It can be especially difficult to litigate an Establishment Clause claim because the applicable law is in a state of flux. *Lemon v. Kurtzman*, 403 U.S. 602 (1971), the seminal case in the area, established a three-part test: government action challenged under the Establishment Clause is unconstitutional unless (1) the government had a secular purpose for its action, (2) the action did not advance or inhibit religion, and (3) the action did not foster excessive entanglement between government and religion. While the *Lemon* test has been roundly criticized by individual members of the Court for failing to accommodate the historical role of religion in public life, it has not been overruled. The Court, however, has declined to apply it in some Establishment Clause cases while continuing to apply it in others. *Cf. Lamb's Chapel v. Center Moriches Union Free School Dist.*, 508 U.S. 384, 398 (1993) (Scalia, J., concurring) ("Like some ghoul in a late-night horror movie that repeatedly sits up in its grave and shuffles abroad, after being repeatedly killed and buried, *Lemon* stalks our Establishment Clause jurisprudence once again, frightening the little children and school attorneys").

Because of dissatisfaction with *Lemon*, different constitutional standards have been applied in certain types of cases. Public funding cases have been analyzed under the doctrine of "neutrality," which enables religious organizations to participate in government programs on the same terms as private organizations. For example, in *Zelman v. Simmons-Harris*, 536 U.S. 639 (2002), Ohio enacted a program intended to aid children in the struggling Cleveland City School District. Among other things, the program allocated state funds for tuition aid to eligible parents of school children. The tuition aid could be used for attendance at specified public and private schools, including religiously-affiliated private schools. The Court found that the tuition aid program was neutral because the same aid was offered regardless of whether the child attended a religious or secular school, and no other aspect of the program either coerced or encouraged parents to send their children to religious schools. *Id.* at 662-63 ("the Ohio program is entirely neutral with respect to religion [because i]t permits [parents] to exercise genuine choice among options public and private, secular and religious.").

Public religious displays, curriculum requirements, and student-initiated prayers have been subject to an "endorsement" test that asks whether a reasonable observer would believe that the government has either approved or disapproved of religion in a way that makes adherence relevant to a person's "standing in the community." *See Wallace v. Jaffree*, 472 U.S. 38 (1985) (Alabama statute mandating one minute of silent meditation at beginning of the school day endorsed religion); *Lynch v. Donnelly*, 465 U.S. 668, 687 (1984) (O'Connor, J., concurring) (government did not endorse religion by erecting a display including "a Santa Claus house, reindeer pulling Santa's sleigh, candy-striped poles, a Christmas tree, carolers, cutout figures representing such characters as a clown, an elephant, and a teddy bear, hundreds of colored lights, a large banner that reads 'SEASONS GREETINGS,' and the crèche"). This test is hard to apply as it depends on a judge's subjective judgment whether a display or other government action sends a message of endorsement. Not surprisingly, then, the Court has reached split decisions on relatively similar religious displays. In *Allegheny v. ACLU*, 492 U.S. 573 (1989), the Court upheld a display that included a menorah, a Christmas tree, and a sign celebrating liberty, while finding endorsement in a free-standing crèche sitting on the inside stairwell of a county courthouse. And in a pair of cases decided on the same day, the Court upheld a Ten Commandments monument placed among 38 other installations on the 22-acre grounds of the Texas State Capitol, while finding impermissible endorsement in posting a text of the Ten Commandments on the walls of two county courthouses. *See McCreary County v. ACLU*, 545 U.S. 844 (2005); *Van Orden v. Perry*, 545 U.S. 677 (2005).

The Court has also applied a "coercion test" to prayer at government functions. For example, the Court has held that prayer at a public high school graduation indirectly coerces participation from non-adherents through the peer pressure of classmates. *Lee v. Weisman*, 505 U.S. 577, 592–93 (1992). The Court applied the same peer pressure coercion rationale to prayer at a high school football game. *Santa Fe Indep. Sch. Dist. v. Doe*, 530 U.S. 290 (2000). No such coercion was found, however, from prayer offered at the opening session of a state legislature. *Marsh v. Chambers*, 463 U.S. 783 (1983).

Practice Tip: Asking whether a particular statute or regulation reflects a government "endorsement" or "coerces" non-adherents to participate in a religious exercise may be another way of asking whether the challenged law has either the "purpose" or "effect" of establishing religion. These tests are in fact a product of the criticism directed at *Lemon*. But *Lemon* has not been overruled, at least not yet, so don't forget to invoke that case when litigating an Establishment Clause claim.

EXERCISE 14

You work for a non-profit advocacy organization and have been asked to testify at an upcoming legislative hearing on whether either of two proposed amendments to a moment of silence statute would, if enacted, violate the Establishment Clause. Both proposals are reprinted below. Italicized text indicates an addition to the previous law; a strike-through indicates a deletion.

Draft an outline of the points you will raise during your testimony, citing relevant case law.

REQUIRED TASKS:

Task 1:   Identify case law relevant to the constitutionality of a classroom moment of silence.

Task 2:   Analyze whether either proposal would violate the Establishment Clause (the LexisNexis Web Course contains clean copies of the proposals without italics or strikeouts).

PRACTICE SKILLS UTILIZED:

Skill 1:   Case research

Skill 2:   Critical reasoning

ESTIMATED TIME FOR COMPLETION: Approximately 45 minutes

LEVEL OF DIFFICULTY (1 TO 5):

PROPOSAL 1:

Teachers shall reserve one minute at the start of each school day for a period of reflection *and reverence* during which time the teacher ~~may~~ *shall*:

(a)   *In the presence of all students in the classroom, recite out loud the Pledge of Allegiance in accordance with Title 4, section 4 of the United States Code.*

~~(a)~~ *(b)*   Instruct students to spend the *remaining* time independently in a ~~silent~~ moment of prayer *or meditation.*

PROPOSAL 2:

Teachers shall reserve one minute at the start of each school day for a period of reflection *and reverence* during which time the teacher ~~may~~ *shall*:

(a) ~~Instruct students to spend the time independently in a silent moment of prayer.~~

(a) *Lead students in a recitation of the Pledge of Allegiance in accordance with Title 4, section 4 of the United States Code.*

(b) *Inform students of their constitutional right to pray in school, and lead willing students who voluntarily choose to participate in a moment of silent prayer.*

Chapter 15

THE FREE EXERCISE CLAUSE

INTRODUCTION

The Free Exercise Clause comes into play when a legal obligation conflicts with the requirements of a given faith. Consider this: should a prohibition on underage drinking apply at a Catholic mass where adherents sip wine as a symbolic representation of the blood of Christ? Should Jews who are not of age be prohibited from drinking wine during the Passover Seder, Purim celebration, or Sabbath ritual? Wine may be a sacred part of these religious ceremonies, but that does not discount the state's interest in controlling underage drinking. Laws such as these prohibit adherents from participating in rituals that are required by their religion. Do they violate the Free Exercise Clause?

What happens in the event of a constitutional conflict? A law that seeks to protect one person's right to equal protection or due process may interfere with another person's right to free exercise. Could a property owner be forced to rent an apartment to a gay or lesbian couple if she believes that doing so is contrary to the laws of God? Must a doctor perform an abortion or a pharmacist fill a birth control prescription against the dictates of their religion?

A challenge to any of these laws would present three common issues: (1) whether the plaintiff has established a genuinely held religious belief; (2) whether the law substantially burdens an exercise of that belief; and (3) what standard of review applies if there is a substantial burden on religion.

The Free Exercise Clause only protects sincerely held religious beliefs, as opposed to other important, though non-religious, personal convictions. The inquiry is largely subjective, and is not concerned with whether the religious belief is reasonable or accepted by mainstream organized faiths. *Thomas v. Review Bd. Ind. Empl. Sec.*, 450 U.S. 707 (1981); *United States v. Ballard*, 322 U.S. 78 (1944). Moreover, the Free Exercise Clause does not apply to a law that simply makes it more difficult to practice religion. In order to trigger constitutional scrutiny, the law must "substantially burden," or effectively coerce, a religious adherent into violating a sincerely held belief. *Lyng v. Northwest Indian Cemetery Protective Ass'n*, 485 U.S. 439 (1988).

Whether such a law is unconstitutional, however, depends on the standard of review that applies in a given case. *Employment Division v. Smith*, 494 U.S. 872 (1990), held that a neutral, generally applicable criminal law that substantially burdens religion will be upheld so long as it is "reasonable." *Cf. Jacobson v. Massachusetts*, 197 U.S. 11 (1905) (rejecting Equal Protection Clause challenge to mandatory state smallpox vaccine). To be "neutral," government action must not

93

target conduct because of its religious motivation. *Church of Lukumi Babalu Aye, Inc. v. Hialeah*, 508 U.S. 520, 532 (1993). To be generally applicable, government action must cover all conduct that threatens the government's interest, and not only conduct with religious motivation. *Id.* at 542-43.

Smith involved a law that was both neutral and generally applicable. There, members of the Native American Church made sacramental use of peyote, which was a prohibited controlled substance under state law. The Court held that the state's peyote ban was both neutral and generally applicable. The law was neutral because it banned peyote use on account of health and safety concerns and not its religious motivation. Further, the law was generally applicable because it covered all peyote use, and not just sacramental use. Applying lesser judicial scrutiny, the Court upheld the peyote ban as a reasonable public health and safety measure. *Id.* at 890.

Three years after *Smith*, the Court struck down a city ordinance in *Church of the Lukumi* that it characterized as non-neutral and not generally applicable. There, a city ordinance effectively prohibited animal slaughter only when performed by members of the Santeria Church as part of their worship service. Thus, the law not only targeted animal slaughter because of its religious motivation, but also only when performed as part of religious worship. *Church of the Lukumi*, 508 U.S. at 546. The Court applied strict scrutiny and struck down the ordinance. *Id.* at 546-47.

While *Smith* established a general rule for Free Exrcise Clause cases, it did not overrule two prior lines of cases that called for greater judicial scrutiny of certain laws that burden religious exercise. First, in *Hobbie v. Unemployment Appeals Commission*, 480 U.S. 136 (1987), and *Sherbert v. Verner*, 374 U.S. 398 (1963), the Court ruled in favor of religious adherents who were disqualified from receiving unemployment benefits after refusing to work on their Sabbath. Second, *Wisconsin v. Yoder*, 406 U.S. 205 (1972), enjoined the enforcement of a compulsory education law against religious adherents. *Smith* noted that *Yoder* involved a "hybrid" rights claim. *Smith*, 494 U.S. at 881-82. That is, the parents in *Yoder* raised two constitutional rights: the right to free exercise of religion combined with the right of a fit parent to direct the education of their child. Strict scrutiny applied in *Hobbie, Sherbert*, and *Yoder*, which meant the government had to prove that the law served a compelling objective that could not be achieved in an alternative, less burdensome way.

Further complicating matters is the tension between the two religion clauses of the First Amendment. In some scenarios, the government's effort to avoid an Establishment Clause violation risks a violation of the Free Exercise Clause, as when government officials prohibit certain religious practices in public school. In *Locke v. Davey*, 540 U.S. 712 (2004), Chief Justice Rehnquist announced that there must be "room for play in the joints" between the religion clauses, and that some state actions might be "permitted by the Establishment Clause, but not required by the Free Exercise Clause." There is no bright line rule for resolving these complicated cases, however.

Practice Tip: Lawmakers can avoid some of these conflicts legislatively. In response to *Smith*, Congress passed the Religious Freedom Restoration Act, which prohibits any substantial burden on religion unless it is the least restrictive means of furthering a compelling interest. Although *Boerne v. Flores*, 521 U.S. 507 (1997), subsequently held that RFRA was an unconstitutional restriction on generally applicable state laws, RFRA nonetheless remains valid as a restriction on generally applicable federal laws. *See Gonzales v. O Centro Espirita Beneficente Uniao do Vegetal*, 546 U.S. 418 (2006). Moreover, a number of states have passed their own 'mini-RFRA' statutes, and the federal government has passed the Religious Land Use and Institutionalized Persons Act, which subjects municipal zoning laws and prison regulations that substantially burden religion to strict scrutiny analysis.

Other statutes also seek to balance free exercise rights with competing interests. Title VII of the Civil Rights Act prohibits various types of employment discrimination but does not apply to certain hiring decisions that would violate the employer's religious obligations. The Fair Housing Act prohibits discrimination in the rental of housing units, but includes a limited exemption for religious organizations and does not even apply to small apartment owners who live in close proximity to tenants. Similarly, most underage drinking and controlled substances laws accommodate at least some religious sacraments. Religious convictions are also being considered as more states move to extend legal protection to gay, lesbian and transgendered persons. Without a statutory or regulatory exemption, however, the Free Exercise Clause may come into play, leaving courts to strike a difficult balance between competing interests.

EXERCISE 15

The state of Astoria enacted a statute that requires females between the ages of 9 and 11 to receive a vaccine against the Human Papilloma Virus [HPV] before they can enroll in public school. The statute was passed in response to a spike in adult onset cervical cancer that scientists believe can be caused by a prior HPV infection. The virus is transmitted from males to females during sexual intercourse, but cannot be passed through casual contact. The FDA-approved vaccine is most effective when administered during adolescence, and is only effective on females. At the time the lawsuit was brought, there was no comparable vaccine for males.

Connor Malloy, a member of the Purist Church, refuses to vaccinate her 10 year old daughter because it would violate her religion. She believes that God has a divine plan for everyone, and that it is a sin to interfere with that plan, even to protect the health of a child.

There are two parts to this exercise.

In Part 1, you represent the State of Astoria and must defend the statute against a Free Exercise challenge. Jonas Barnette, another member of the Purist Church, has been deposed, and an affidavit from Dr. Rosalyn Kane has been received. Based on the testimony these witnesses could provide at trial, should you: (a) challenge the sincerity of the plaintiff's religious beliefs, (b) challenge the asserted burden on religion, or (c) concede these issues and defend the statute under the appropriate substantive standard of review? Be prepared to explain your answers.

In Part 2, you represent the challenger, Connor Malloy, and must respond to the state's summary judgment motion. At this point in the proceedings, no relevant facts are in dispute. You must therefore decide whether to challenge the merits of the statute under *Smith*, or attempt to establish that a different line of cases applies.

(PART 1) ESTIMATED TIME: Approximately 45 minutes

Task 1:   Identify facts obtained through discovery that will be useful in defending against a Free Exercise challenge.

Skill 1:   Factual development

(PART 2) ESTIMATED TIME: Approximately 1 hour

Task 2:	Draft a Memorandum in Opposition to Defendant's Motion for Summary Judgment (the LexisNexis Web Course contains a form for the memorandum that has been started for you).
Skill 2:	Critical reasoning
Skill 3:	Motion drafting

LEVEL OF DIFFICULTY (1 TO 5):

UNITED STATES DISTRICT COURT
FOR THE DISTRICT OF ASTORIA

Connor Malloy, 　　　　　Plaintiff 　　　　　　v. State of Astoria, 　　　　　Defendant	C.A. No. 08-5247 January 15

TRANSCRIBED DEPOSITION EXCERPTS

Court Reporter: Stephen Jones, RMR
                               Court Reporters, Inc.
                               527 Main Street
                               Princeton, Astoria 52248

Plaintiff's Attorney: Stephen Maillard
                               Maillard, Stern and Root, LLC
                               14 North Smithfield Road
                               Princeton, Astoria 52248

Defense Attorney: Kaley Samuels
                               State Attorney General's Office
                               224 Franklin View Parkway
                               Albertson, Astoria 52241

Court Reporters, Inc.
527 Main Street
Princeton, Astoria 52248

Proceedings

(Deposition Excerpt of Jonas Barnette)

Q.   Please state your name and age.

A.   My name is Jonas Barnette and I am 38 years old.

Q.   Tell us your address and how long you've lived there.

A.   I live at 1429 Rice Lane in Acadia, and I've lived there all my life.

Q.   Are you employed?

A.   Well, not technically, but I spend most of my time doing things related to the church.

Q.   Do you mean the Purist Church?

A.   Yes, I do.

Q.   For how long have you been involved with the church?

A.   For the past 25 years, ever since I was 13 years old.

Q. Why did you get involved?

A. My parents started the religion on their own around the time I turned 13. We used to be Catholic, but they disagreed with many of the mainstream teachings and wanted to live by the true laws of God.

Q. How many followers belong to the Purist Church?

A. Right now we have 37 members, mostly aunts, uncles, cousins, grandparents and the like. We share the same values about God and how to live a good life on earth. A couple years ago we tried recruiting new members. We put an ad in the local paper inviting members of the community to a weekly service at my parent's house. No one showed up so I guess they're not too interested in what we're doing.

Q. What is your role in the Church as a child of the founders and now its leader?

A. Well, I lead church services and sometimes people come to me with questions about how to live a life that is pleasing to God. I try to give them good advice.

Q. So you're the church leader?

A. Well, we don't really have a leader officially. But family members come to me because I know more about what my parents thought of God than anyone else.

Q. How do you know what is "pleasing to God?" Do you look to the Bible, Quran or some other religious text?

A. No. God spoke to my parents in a series of dreams and they recorded those conversations in The Book of Purist Teachings. The advice I give is based on the Book.

Q. Does the Book of Purist Teachings say anything about child vaccinations?

A. Not expressly, no.

Q. What do you mean, not expressly?

A. God told my parents that "In the afterlife, you will be called to account for every decision you make on earth. As parents, you must not harm your children in any way, for those who do are not worthy of a life in Heaven."

Q. How does this relate to vaccinations?

A. Well, it means that parents must keep their children safe if they want to enter the kingdom of Heaven. If a vaccination can ward off a disease, then the decision not to vaccinate puts the child at harm. Parents who don't vaccinate won't go to Heaven. I was vaccinated and I don't think my parents would have done that had they thought it was against God's law.

Q. Do other members of your church believe the same thing?

A.   Well, I've never talked to anyone about vaccines specifically it's not something that's important to us one way or the other. I mean, yes, the Book says that a parent who harms a child cannot enter Heaven, and faced with a choice of giving a safe vaccine and leaving your child exposed to a disease in the future, it makes sense that you'd have to give the vaccine. But it's not something parents can't disagree on, I suppose. It doesn't mean you're kicked out of the family if you don't want to give a vaccine.

End Transcript

Dr. Rosalyn Kane

8822 State University Road, College Town, Astoria 11221; (822) 539–7349

RE: *Connor Malloy v. State of Astoria*, Affidavit of Dr. Rosalyn Kane

I, Rosalyn Kane, under penalty of perjury, do testify and swear:

1. I am over 18 years of age and competent to testify on the matters herein set forth. I make this affidavit based on my own personal knowledge.

2. I graduated from Yale Divinity School with a Ph.D. in Comparative Religion in 1982. Between 1982 and 1985 I was a Senior Research Analyst with the United Nations Economic, Social and Cultural Organization, where I researched the position of dozens of religious organizations as it relates to medical issues and the treatment of diseases. My specific focus was on new and emerging religions that are less than 50 years old. I have been employed as a faculty member at State University since 1985 where I teach several courses on Comparative Religious Practices. I have written over 35 articles on this topic, all of which have been published in peer-reviewed journals. I belong to the Association of University Professors, the Institute for Comparative Religious Studies, and Chair the University's Committee on Religious Diversity.

3. I was asked by Attorney Kaley Samuels to provide information on the teachings of the Purist Church as they relate to physical health issues generally and childhood vaccines in particular. Prior to Ms. Samuels' inquiry, I was not aware of the existence of the Purist Church.

4. I have sought to obtain information on the Purist Church and its teachings using generally accepted research methods, including consultation with on-line subscription databases, professional journals, and other religious studies experts. None of these sources provided information about the Purist Church.

5. No religious organization that has emerged within the past 50 years adheres to a view that it is a sin to vaccinate a child against the risk of future disease. Among the hundreds of established religions I have studied over the course of my career, only the most extreme and irrational denominations take this view. Even the Jehovah's Witnesses, known for their strong religious opposition to outside medical treatment, do not believe that it is a sin to vaccinate a child.

6. The Federal Tax Code exempts qualified charities, including religious organizations, from having to pay federal taxes. In response to Ms. Samuels' inquiry, I consulted the appropriate IRS database and found that The Purist Church is not exempt.

7. I declare under the penalty of perjury that the foregoing is true and correct to the best of my knowledge.

Dated, September 2

College Town, Astoria

Dr. Rosalyn Kane

Rosalyn Kane, Ph.D.

UNITED STATES DISTRICT COURT FOR THE DISTRICT OF ASTORIA

Connor Malloy,
            Plaintiff
               v.

State of Astoria,
            Defendant

C.A. No. 08-5247
January 15

Defendant's Motion for Summary Judgment

I. Astoria Is Not Required To Recognize a Religious Exemption From a Neutral and Generally Applicable Childhood Vaccine Requirement That Reasonably Furthers a Legitimate Health Objective

Employment Department v. Smith, 494 U.S. 872 (1990), held that the Free Exercise Clause does not require the state to exempt religious adherents from neutral, generally applicable laws. The vaccination requirement falls into this category.

Plaintiff has not alleged that the vaccine statute was enacted to burden a particular religious group. Nor could she. The statute was passed after state health officials documented a rise in cervical cancer caused by a virus that spreads through sexual intercourse. The legislature did not even know about the Purist Church until after the law was passed.

The law requires all females within the covered age group to show proof of vaccination before enrolling in school, but allows a parent who objects to the vaccination to seek an exemption by making a "good cause" showing to a designated health official. The state has granted an exemption when the vaccine would exacerbate a pre-existing medical condition, or when a doctor's office or clinic has exhausted its vaccine supply prior to the start of the school year. Purists are entitled to claim an exemption for these reasons to the same extent as any other public school students.

II. Prayer For Relief

Because the statute is a neutral, generally applicable law that furthers a legitimate health objective as described in *Smith*, its enforcement against members of the Purist Church does not violate the Free Exercise Clause. Summary judgment in favor of the Defendant is therefore appropriate.

Kevin Jones

Attorney Kevin Jones (Astoria #55497)
Assistant Attorney General
State of Astoria